GOLD STARS
OVER THE RED RIVER

GOLD STARS
OVER THE RED RIVER

The Fighter Regiments And The Aces Of
The Vietnam People's Air Force

Kirk R. Lowry

So Việt Edition
ℛ **Aviation That Guards Press** ★
Toronto

So Việt Edition
Aviation That Guards Press
232 Blackthorn Avenue
Toronto, Ontario M6N 3H8

Fourth printing, expanded edition, 2020
ISBN 9798648643956

Cover design by Patricia Yu

Photograph sources: page 12, Kirk R. Lowry, pages 80-102,
Dr. István Toperczer, page 218, Kirk R. Lowry

The front cover painting by Michael Turner depicts
Mikoyan-Gurevich MiG-21PFL 4326 serial 772111 being flown to
intercept a Republic F-105. The very event occurred on 18
November 1967 when Nguyen Van Coc of the 921st Fighter
Regiment, flying MiG-21PFL 4326, having gained an advantage of height,
fired an R-3S missile causing the destruction of Republic F-105D
60-0497 flown by William N. Reed of the 469th Tactical Fighter
Squadron, 388th Tactical Fighter Wing. Reed was able to eject over the
Kingdom of Laos and be rescued. Coc went on to become the highest
scoring of the aces of the American War with 9 victories confirmed.

On the frontispiece is a poster that was created in the Democratic
Republic of Vietnam to celebrate the success of THE MAN OF THE
HA TAY REGION [which is located by the Red River] THE HERO NGUYEN
DUC SOAT WHO USED 6 MISSILES TO DESTROY 6 U.S. AIRCRAFT.

On the rear cover are posters which were created in the Democratic
Republic of Vietnam during the American War to extoll the Air Defence
Forces and the Vietnam People's Air Force; that on the upper left calls
for CELEBRATION OF THE GLORIOUS FEAT OF THE PEOPLE OF THE
NORTH IN SHOOTING DOWN 1,500 U.S. AIRCRAFT, that on the upper
right notes THE SHARP EDGED VICTORY, the lower poster recognizes
the PROTECTION OF THE TERRITORY OF SOCIALIST VIETNAM.

Dedication

This work is dedicated
to the courageous women, children and men
who worked and fought to liberate, defend and unite
Vietnam

Contents

Preface

I first learned of the Fighter Regiments and the aces of the Vietnam People's Air Force when, as a reward for a summer long commitment to yard work of the most bothersome sort, my father gave a book. Fighter Aces. Published and received in 1975, the volume contained fascinating accounts about pilots in combat written by Christopher Shores and included wonderful paintings of aerial engagements by Michael Turner.

The apocryphal facts about Vietnamese pilots and the evocative painting of a MiG-21 of the Vietnam People's Air Force included in the book were enough to create interest which germinated gradually over time into obsession. However, it was not until a visit to the Air Defence - Air Force Museum in Hanoi that the notion of writing a book of some sort about the Vietnamese who took to the air to defend their country was considered. Now, after what seemed an eternity, suddenly, a book has been written.

What the Vietnamese call the American War remains a divisive event about which the diversity of opinion is vast. Much has been written about the conflict and much will be written about the strife that engulfed Vietnam and affected so many both within and without the country, but, Gold Stars Over The Red River examines a specific aspect of the conflict, that being, the aerial operations to defend the Democratic Republic of Vietnam. Essentially a work of two parts, the volume includes a history of the Fighter Regiments of the Vietnam People's Air Force and a record of the claims of those pilots who may be described as aces.

Gold Stars Over The Red River details the struggle between the Vietnam People's Air Force and the American air forces from the Vietnamese perspective, not so as to be contentious but, rather, to complement research undertaken by writers describing the American perspective of the events. The study of aerial combat past has been progressive. In the immediate aftermath of conflicts information is restricted to but a few and legend becomes rife among many but the patience and perseverance of the dedicated has meant that facts, existent but unknown, are revealed over time as, for example, any student of Great War aviation knows and celebrates. Significant intelligence has been made public about the efforts of the American air forces which flew over Vietnam, however, until recently, knowledge of the force which flew in defence of the Democratic Republic of Vietnam was scant. Dr. István Toperczer, who published a history of the Vietnam People's Air Force, Air War Over North Vietnam, in 1998, established contact with veterans of the service and gained access to official records. The collecting of a trove of information has resulted in the publication of several fascinating books about the subject which have made possible the writing of Gold Stars Over The Red River.

Others, as well, have written invaluable sources of information and evaluation relevant to the writing of a work about the subject. Data compiled by Yefim Gordon with colleagues Keith Dexter and Dmitriy Komissarov describing aircraft operated by the Vietnam People's Air Force in both technical and operational detail were essential aids. Analysis by Marshall L. Michel III was fundamental to the understanding of the effects of operations undertaken to defend the Democratic Republic of Vietnam.

I also, gratefully, acknowledge Dr. István Toperczer for providing, with true socialist generosity, the photographs with which this work is illustrated.

Michael Turner is given thanks, in recognition of both the talent possessed and the kindness extended, for allowing the use on the cover of the very painting which first aroused interest in the subject of Gold Stars Over The Red River.

I am so appreciative of the work done by Patricia Yu who graciously offered labour and expertise and designed such a beautiful cover.

Betty Lowry and Ron Lowry, my mother and father, who first inspired an interest in writing and aviation, respectively, who consistently supported free thinking and recognized the courage of conviction, who always gave support, are thanked and ever remembered with love.

Others, too, have been of great help while the research and writing were done. Mike Felix read a manuscript of the text and offered suggestions. Gratitude is expressed to Natalie Kong-Foon who helped to preserve the peaceful environment in which the work could be done and was never heard to complain about piles of books constantly being shifted about or anything else for that matter.   My son, René Lowry, who happened to be studying various aspects of Vietnamese history in the process of obtaining a university degree while I was researching and writing, is thanked for provoking illuminating insights and offering the support of one who has endured the horror of a screen blazing white when bare of words and also for suggesting the occasional respite to be provided by those Red Letter types.

Love, respect and appreciation are felt for and given to Stephanie Chiu, a comrade for all seasons. As we have travelled she has consistently been enthusiastic in the search for aircraft and patient once aircraft were found.   Stephanie always offered support and encouragement while information was compiled and writing was done to complete Gold Stars Over The Red River and played a role significant in the editing and printing of the work. Our return, together, to Vietnam is eagerly anticipated.

Stephanie stands by the favourite MiG, actually Shenyang   J-6 6058 serial 6436, of the 925th Fighter Regiment at the Air Defence - Air Force Museum in Hanoi.

Nomenclature

One who studies the history of the Vietnam People's Air Force using sources written in the English language faces the daunting task of recognizing the numerous and complex names of both individuals and aircraft. The repetition of some, for example, Nguyen or MiG, makes for tiresome reading. Apologies are given in advance.

Diacritics have not been used on either Vietnamese place names or people's names in the body of the text which are, therefore, written using the English alphabet and manner.

Generally Vietnamese names consist of three parts; first is the surname, following is a middle name, third is the given name. People are referred to by the given name both personally and professionally. Thus, the first pilot of a Fighter Regiment of the Vietnam People's Air Force to claim a victory, Pham Ngoc Lan, would commonly be known as Lan both casually and formally.

The exception to the standard is Ho Chi Minh who became so famous as to be known by surname and was commonly referred to, with affection, as Uncle Ho.

Many Vietnamese have the same surname and it is common for people to have the same name in entirety as, for example, did two pilots who each became famous flying with the Vietnam People's Air Force known as Nguyen Van Bay.

Aircraft are commonly identified by the abbreviated designation used by the manufacturer in the text. Thus a Mikoyan-Gurevich MiG-17 is noted as a MiG-17. Versions of aircraft licence built, or otherwise built outside of the country of design, are specified only when certain to have been such, therefore a version of the MiG-17 known to have been built in the People's Republic of China is identified as a Shenyang J-5 while a MiG-17 of unknown manufacture is described as a MiG-17.

It is sincerely hoped that the reader is not daunted by the nomenclature.

14

Acronyms And Initialisms

The Democratic Republic of Vietnam and the United States of America, while administered by different political systems, both created significant bureaucracies. In the perpetual effort of such organizations to be efficient, appellations were reduced to acronyms and initialisms. Those in the text, official in origin, or technical in derivation, have been listed.

AAA - anti aircraft artillery
AAM - air to air missile
ACS - Air Commando Squadron
ACW - Air Commando Wing
ADF - Air Defence Forces
ADF-VPAF - Air Defence Forces of the Vietnam People's Air Force
ARRS - Aerospace Rescue and Recovery Service
ARVN - Army of the Republic of Vietnam
CAP - combat air patrol
CIA - Central Intelligence Agency
CR - Czechoslovak Republic
CSG - Combat Support Group
DK - Democratic Kampuchea
DPRK - Democratic People's Republic of Korea
DRV - Democratic Republic of Vietnam
ECM - electronic counter measure
EWO - Electronic Warfare Officer
FR - French Republic
FW - Fighter Wing
GCI - ground controlled interception
IF - Indochinese Federation
KL - Kingdom of Laos
KR - Khmer Republic
KT - Kingdom of Thailand
MAAG - Military Assistance and Advisory Group
NLFSV - National Liberation Front for South Vietnam
PRC - People's Republic of China
RC - Republic of Cuba
RIO - Radar Intercept Officer
RVN - Republic of Vietnam
SAM - surface to air missile
SAR - search and rescue
TEWS - Tactical Electronic Warfare Squadron
TFS - Tactical Fighter Squadron
TFW - Tactical Fighter Wing
TRW - Tactical Reconnaissance Wing
USA - United States of America
USAF - United States Air Force
USMC - United States Marine Corps
USN - United States Navy
USSR - Union of Soviet Socialist Republics
VA - Navy Attack Squadron
VF - Navy Fighter Squadron
VFP - Navy Light Photographic Squadron
VNAF - Vietnamese Air Force
VPA - Vietnam People's Army
VPAF - Vietnam People's Air Force
WSO - Weapons Systems Operator

Aircraft Referred To In The Text

Aircraft Operated By Air America, The Republic of China Air Force, The United States Air Force, The United States Marine Corps, The United States Navy And The Vietnamese Air Force

A-1 - The Douglas A-1 Skyraider, a single radial piston engined, single seat tactical attack aircraft operated by the USAF, the USN and the VNAF.

A-4 - The Douglas A-4 Skyhawk, a single turbojet engined, single seat tactical attack aircraft operated by the USMC and the USN.

A-6 - The Grumman A-6 Intruder, a two turbojet engined, two seat tactical attack aircraft operated by the USMC and the USN.

A-7 - The Vought A-7 Corsair II, a single turbofan engined, single seat tactical attack aircraft operated by the USAF and the USN.

AQM-34 - The Ryan AQM-34 Firebee, a single turbojet engined, reconnaissance drone operated by the USAF.

B-52 - The Boeing B-52 Stratofortress, a eight turbofan engined, six seat strategic bomber operated by the USAF.

C-47 - The Douglas C-47 Skytrain, a two radial piston engined, two seat (or more) transport operated by the USAF.

C-123 - The Fairchild C-123 Provider, a two radial piston engined, two seat tactical transport operated by Air America and the Republic of China Air Force, at the behest of the CIA, and the VNAF.

CH-3 - The Sikorsky CH-3 Jolly Green Giant, a two turboshaft, two seat (or more) transport helicopter operated by the USAF.

EB-66 - The Douglas EB-66 Destroyer, a two turbojet engined, three seat electronic counter measure aircraft operated by the USAF.

F-4 - The McDonnell Douglas F-4 Phantom II, a two turbojet engined, two seat fighter and bomber operated the USAF, the USMC and the USN.

F-8 - The Vought F-8 Crusader, a single turbojet engined, single seat fighter aircraft operated by the USN.

F-100 - The North American F-100 Super Sabre, a single turbojet engined, single seat fighter and bomber operated by the USAF.

F-101 - The McDonnell F-101 Voodoo, a two turbojet engined, two seat fighter operated by the USAF.

F-102 - The Convair F-102 Delta Dagger, a single turbojet engined, single seat fighter operated by the USAF.

F-105 - The Republic F-105 Thunderchief, a single turbojet engined fighter and bomber operated, in single seat and two seat versions, by the USAF.

F-111 - The General Dynamics F-111 Aardvark, a two turbofan engined, two seat bomber operated by the USAF.

HH-53 - The Sikorsky HH-53 Super Jolly Green Giant, a two turboshaft, six seat transport helicopter operated by the USAF.

KC-135 - The Boeing KC-135 Stratotanker, a four turbojet engined, four seat tanker and transport operated by the USAF.

O-2 - The Cessna O-2 Skymaster, a two flat piston engined, two seat utility aircraft operated by the USAF.

OV-10 - The North American OV-10 Bronco, a two turbo engined, two seat tactical attack aircraft operated by the USAF.

RA-5 - The North American RA-5 Vigilante, a two turbojet engined, two seat reconnaissance aircraft operated by the USN.

RC-47 - The Douglas RC-47, a two radial piston engined, two seat (or more) electronic intelligence gathering aircraft operated by the USAF.

RF-4 - The McDonnell Douglas RF-4 Phantom II, a two turbojet engined, two seat reconnaissance aircraft operated the USAF and the USMC.

RF-8 - The Vought RF-8 Crusader, a single turbojet engined, single seat reconnaissance aircraft operated by the USMC and the USN.

RF-101 - The McDonnell RF-101 Voodoo, a two turbojet engined, two seat reconnaissance aircraft operated by the USAF.

Aircraft Operated By The Vietnam People's Air Force

A-37 - Cessna A-37 Dragonfly, a two turbojet engined, two seat tactical attack aircraft.

CJ-6 - The Nanchang CJ-6, a single radial piston engined, two seat trainer.

F-5 - The Northrop F-5 Freedom Fighter, a two turbojet engined, single seat fighter.

FT-5 - Shenyang FT-5, a single turbojet engined, two seat trainer.

IL-28 - Ilyushin IL-28, a two turbojet engined, three seat bomber.

J-5 - Shenyang J-5, a licence built version of the Mikoyan-Gurevich MiG-17, single turbojet engined, single seat fighter.

J-6 - Shenyang J-6, a licence built version of the Mikoyan-Gurevich MiG-19, two turbojet engined, single seat fighter.

JJ-2 - Shenyang JJ-2, a licence built version of the Mikoyan-Gurevich MiG-15UTI, single turbojet engined, two seat trainer.

Li-2 - The Lisunov Li-2, a licence built version of the Douglas DC-3, two radial piston engined, five seat (or more) transport.

Mi-4 - The Mil Mi-4, a radial piston engined, three seat, transport helicopter.

Mi-6 - The Mil Mi-6, a two turboshaft, five seat, transport helicopter.

MiG-15 - The Mikoyan-Gurevich MiG-15, a single turbojet engined, single seat fighter.

MiG-15UTI - The Mikoyan-Gurevich MiG-15UTI, a single turbojet engined, two seat trainer.

MiG-17 - The Mikoyan-Gurevich MiG-17, a single turbojet engined, single seat fighter.

MiG-19 - The Mikoyan-Gurevich MiG-19, a two turbojet engined, single seat fighter.

MiG-21 - The Mikoyan-Gurevich MiG-21, a single turbojet engined, single seat fighter.

T-28 - The North American T-28 Trojan, a single radial piston engined, two seat trainer.

Z.226T - The Zlin 226T Trener-6, a single in line piston engined, two seat trainer.

Claims

Though of no significance to the soldiers, sailors and civilians subjected to aerial attack, the claims made by pilots to have shot down aircraft have been and remain the primary subject of interest to historians of conflict in the air.   Despite intensive study, much about who accomplished what remains indefinite and that is true about the pilots who claimed aerial victories during the American War.   Flying aircraft at great speed and firing weapons from distant range while manoeuvring through the air and staring through canopies of limited visibility meant that what pilots believed had happened was not necessarily so.

To have a claimed victory confirmed in the Vietnam People's Air Force strict conditions had to be met.   The MiG-17 and MiG-19 were equipped with cameras which automatically shot when the cannons were fired, but a witness of the action or physical evidence of a destroyed aircraft had to be provided in addition to photographic substantiation for a pilot to be credited with a victory.   Pilots of versions of the MiG-21, for which the primary, if not only weapon, utilized was the air to air missile, required that a victory claimed was corroborated by one who saw the action or the discovery of wreckage.

The criteria required to establish just who was to receive credit for an aerial victory was not constant and evolved over time.   Socialist ardour resulted in a policy whereby all pilots who participated in a combat in which it was believed that an aircraft was destroyed were to be deemed as victors but concern for accuracy meant that only the pilot directly responsible for the destruction of an aircraft would be accredited with the success.   Nonetheless, a method of absolute consistency does not appear to have been applied in the compilation of claims by all of the Fighter Regiments of the Vietnam People's Air Force.

Apparently, victories claimed were allotted by staff of the Fighter Regiment to which a pilot was assigned following which an official victory would be recognized after a review of combat reports from all relevant sources, providing the necessary criteria was met, by staff of the Air

Defence Forces of the Vietnam People's Air Force. It was to be expected that a pilot would have more claims than official victories. The idiosyncrasies of the command of each Fighter Regiment affected how victories were recognized as, for example, the 921st Fighter Regiment seldom awarded a single claim to more than one pilot, whereas, the 923rd Fighter Regiment often awarded a victory to all who participated in an action resulting in a claim. The official victory totals noted are those recorded in Những Trận Không Chiến Trên Bầu Trời Việt Nam (1965-1975) Nhìn Từ Hai Phía by Nguyễn Sỹ Hưng and Nguyễn Nam Liên. All claims by a pilot, made in cooperation or individually, that have been identified appear on the listing following an individual biography.

Establishing exactly what happened as a result of aerial battles over the Democratic Republic of Vietnam is made particularly difficult for, despite the rigorous confirmation process, many of the claims of the destruction of an aircraft were made with conviction, but, in error. The total of victories attributed to the pilots of the Fighter Regiments of the Vietnam People's Air Force is in excess of the number of aircraft actually lost by the American air forces as a result of aerial combat. An attempt has been made to establish the veracity of claimed victories, yet, conducting such research has been and will forever be difficult.

A simple comparison of Vietnamese claims with American losses does not necessarily resolve an enquiry as the American pilots were subject to attack from anti aircraft fire and surface to air missiles in addition to aerial interception and identifying the cause of the destruction of an aircraft was and remains difficult. After action reports compiled by the American air forces attempted to conclude just what precipitated a loss but doing so with accuracy was not always possible. That the majority of weapons systems used against the American aircraft were fired from a remote source out of sight to the crew of the target destroyed or of a crew witness to a target struck could make determining the reason for the loss challenging.

Study of the subject reveals another obstacle to the accurate reporting of the aerial combat over the Democratic Republic of Vietnam; in general the American air forces were loathe to attribute the loss of an aircraft to an enemy pilot and any other cause was deemed preferable and, therefore, when possible, was considered probable.

A Brief History Of
The Fighter Regiments

Introduction

The United States of America (USA) began to demonstrate concern for the skies over the Democratic Republic of Vietnam (DRV) in November 1950 when the Military Assistance and Advisory Group (MAAG), which oversaw aid from America to the Indochinese Federation (IF), formed an Air Force Section. The government of the IF, which utilized military forces provided by the French Republic (FR), had been fighting the League for the Independence of Vietnam, known as the Viet Minh, overtly since November 1946. The Air Force Section of the MAAG managed efforts to support the IF which would eventually assume significance in the protracted struggle.

Nonetheless, the French military in Indochina was ultimately defeated following which came the signing of the Geneva Agreements of July 1954 that resulted in Vietnam being recognized as independent, but divided into two parts, the north governed as the DRV and the south governed as the Republic of Vietnam (RVN). A condition of the accord was the reunification of the nation following national elections to be held in 1956, but, refusing to discuss future elections with the government of the DRV, the government of the RVN renounced and breached the Geneva Agreements. The RVN received support from the USA which came in many forms and one form, of profound consequence for the people of the DRV, was aerial.

Following the creation of the National Liberation Front for South Vietnam (NLFSV) on 20 December 1960 and the beginning of an insurgency against the government of the RVN, the role of the MAAG in Vietnamese affairs increased and the incidents real and imagined involving units of the United States Navy (USN) used to support covert attacks on the DRV involving the Central Intelligence Agency (CIA) in the Gulf of Tonkin prompted direct intervention by the USA to begin the American War, with Americans fighting not only throughout the RVN but over the DRV as well. Empowered by an act of the Congress, President Lyndon Johnson, authorized a program of air strikes against targets in the DRV, named Operation Pierce Arrow, which was conducted on 5 August 1964 upon naval facilities and oil reserves. While the defences of the DRV against aerial attack were limited to anti aircraft artillery (AAA), two aircraft were downed, a Douglas A-1 Skyraider and a Douglas A-4 Skyhawk, the pilot of the former, Richard C. Sather, was killed and the pilot of the latter, Everett Alvarez Jr., was made a prisoner of war.

Thus began the painful torment of the American air forces over Vietnam.

Further aerial assaults upon the DRV came after significant American casualties were inflicted following a NLFSV attack upon Camp Holloway. Operation Flaming Dart was authorized and then launched on 7 February 1965 with air strikes by the USN, the United States Air Force (USAF) and the Vietnamese Air Force (VNAF) on concentrations of the Vietnam People's Army (VPA) thought to have aided the NLFSV. Evidently two VNAF A-1s were downed by AAA as was a USN A-4, the pilot of which, Edward A. Dickson, was killed. Undeterred, the NLFSV struck at American soldiers based in Qui Nhon which resulted in a reprisal on 11 February. VPA barracks were attacked at the cost of two USN aircraft, a Vought F-8 Crusader downed by AAA, the pilot of which, Robert H. Shumaker, was made a prisoner of war and an A-4 downed by undetermined causes with the pilot, William T. Majors recovered and, apparently, a VNAF A-1 was downed by AAA as well.   While damage was certainly inflicted, the primary reason for the raids was to convince the leadership of the VPA to cease assisting the NLFSV while bringing about a negotiated end to hostilities.

In the USA the Joint Chiefs of Staff proposed a sustained campaign of aerial assault upon the DRV to interdict supplies sent to, and discourage personnel aiding, the NLFSV. A list of targets was compiled to be struck by the USAF and the USN with the intention of launching two attacks a week for a period of eight weeks under the name Rolling Thunder. Johnson assented to the request on 13 February and, thus, the American War was escalated. Though scheduled to begin on 20 February a coup in the RVN caused delay and Rolling Thunder was initiated on 2 March by units of the USAF and the VNAF, which lost five aircraft to AAA. The raids continued and aircraft continued to be downed which prompted modifications to tactics to reduce the effectiveness of the mass of weapons firing skyward. To limit the possibility of aircraft being struck by AAA it was decided to have pilots approach targets at an altitude of, at the least, 25,000 feet (7620 metres) then dive to launch or drop the carried ordinance below 10,000 feet (3048 metres) then pull up before reaching 4,500 feet (1372 metres).

The skies above the DRV were defended by the Air Defence Forces (ADF) using a vast array of weapons with which to dissuade and destroy attackers. Radar controlled artillery was and would remain the primary means of defence throughout the American War. However, two weapons systems would be introduced following the commencement of Rolling Thunder to great and deadly effect.

3 April was a day of strikes against bridges with Thanh Hoa Bridge, which enabled passage over the Song Ma River by railway and road, known as the Ham Rong, the target of the USAF while the USN attacked other bridges in the vicinity. Protecting A-4s attacking Dong Phong Thuong bridge, two F-8 pilots dove to attack AAA emplacements and then climbed to an altitude of 10,000 feet (3048 metres) when the F-8 flown by Spence Thomas was suddenly struck by cannon shells from behind! With afterburner activated, the aircraft flew away at the highest possible speed.

Having been hit in the vertical tail and both wings and with damage to the utility hydraulics, Thomas was flying an aircraft that could not safely return to an aircraft carrier. It was deemed that Da Nang airfield, used by the USAF and the VNAF, was a safe place to land. Using skill, and an emergency air system to lower the landing gear, Thomas was able to make a landing without injury.

For the first time an American aircraft had been driven from the sky by the Vietnam People's Air Force (VPAF).

Red Star

The aerial interception of aircraft attacking the DRV became a possibility following the establishment of the 921st Red Star Fighter Regiment under the command of Dao Dinh Luyen on 3 February 1964. The pilots had trained in the People's Republic of China (PRC). The four Mikoyan-Gurevich MiG-15UTIs and the 32 Mikoyan-Gurevich MiG-17s to be flown were presented as a gift by the Union of Soviet Socialist Republics (USSR).

The history of aviation in Vietnam saw the establishment of commercial routes and military bases throughout the region. Though the first Vietnamese pilot, Do Huu Vi, began pilot training in 1910 he would never fly in the homeland and would die as an infantry officer having, during The Great War, served with French observation and bombardment units prior to suffering grievous injuries in a crash and transferred to 1 Regiment, French Foreign Legion to be killed in 1916 fighting by the Somme. While the aircraft and pilots and passengers of many nations had flown over the country such service and activity had been beyond the experience of the people of Vietnam.

The intent to form a Vietnamese air force, one element of the efforts to liberate Vietnam, had been decided upon by Vo Nguyen Giap, Chief Commander of the Ministry of Defence, Hoang Van Thai, Chief of Staff, Phan Phac, Chief of Military Training and Ho Chi Minh, President of the DRV, in 1949 and, as a result, the Air Force Research Committee was founded on 9 March. The immediate demands of the struggle for independence prevented the progressive development of an aerial military service and, while organizations and associations relating to the development of military aviation were created, it was not 1959 that the first units of the VPAF were formed; the 919th Air Transport Regiment on 1 May and the 910th Training Regiment on 30 September. Aircraft were adorned with an insignia, based upon the flag of the DRV, consisting of a gold star upon a red roundel over a red bar both of which were surrounded by a gold border.

Much assistance had been given by the Czechoslovak Republic (CR) and the PRC, particularly, in respect of the formation of training schools and the supply of aircraft. The principal training aircraft used were the Zlin-226T Trener-6, from the CR and the Nanchang CJ-6 from the PRC. Students were sent to the CR, the PRC and the USSR to be trained and for many the goal was learning to fly the MiG-17 and, for some, piloting the Mikoyan-Gurevich MiG-21.

Simultaneously, work was undertaken to modify existing airfields and develop new facilities. Support staff had to be trained to service aircraft and operate systems on the ground. The creation of an air force was a daunting task for the DRV.

On 22 October 1963 a unified command structure was organized incorporating the VPAF and the ADF under the command of Phung The Tai to be known as the Air Defence Forces of the Vietnam People's Air Force (ADF-VPAF), thus, facilitating cooperation between AAA, radar, surface to air missile (SAM) systems and aircraft following which an initial aerial victory utilizing the integrated systems was claimed on 16 February 1964. Ordered into the air in response to a radar detection of an unidentified aircraft flying along the frontier with the Kingdom of Laos (KL) , Nguyen Van Ba and Le Tien Phuoc, flying a North American T-28 Trojan, took off shortly after 0100 hours and encountered a Fairchild C-123 Provider operated by the VNAF engaged on covert reconnaissance, apparently at the behest of the CIA, which could be seen flying over a cloud in the darkness. The target was fired upon but confirmation of the destruction of the aircraft came only with the interrogation of a soldier of the Army of the Republic of Vietnam (ARVN) some time later.

Following commencement of construction on 1 May 1960, with great effort, and assistance from the PRC, the Phuc Yen airbase, also referred to as Noi Bai, was made able to receive jet powered aircraft in 1964. On 6 August, the very day following the first aerial strikes by American forces against the DRV, project X-1, the posting of the 921st Fighter Regiment to the homeland was initiated and four flights of four MIG-17s took to the air in succession from the airbase by Mengzi in the PRC. The 16 pilots, under the command of Dao Dinh Luyen, landed at Phuc Yen to be greeted by military commanders and, after the ceremony to mark the arrival of the 921st Fighter Regiment, two pairs of aircraft were placed on alert.

A Fighter Regiment was to consist of three Companies each made up of three flights; a flight was to be of four aircraft, a Company of 12 aircraft and a Fighter Regiment of, at least, 36 aircraft. Both pilots and aircraft were available in but limited number and such a situation was to continue throughout the American War, consequently, men in the machines were to be deployed in flights and in pairs. Expediency was the order of each and every day and the result was that aircraft were to be dispersed as necessary and pilots flew missions as dictated by logistics.

On 11 November dignitaries of the DRV inspected the 921st Fighter Regiment which, from Phuc Yen, was to defend the Red River delta, so rich in resources and replete with economic activity in Hanoi and Haiphong, from aggressors. Leading the inspection was Ho Chi Minh. Uncle Ho well understood the importance of morale and spoke enthusiastically to the members of the unit stating

The Vietnamese way of warfare is distinctive. Even a rudimentary weapon becomes effective in the hands of the Vietnamese. We should exploit it and should not fear that the enemy has much more modern weaponry[1].

Yet the men of the unit faced significant difficulties. Prolonged theoretical study and instruction in training aircraft was beneficial but flying experience in the type to be flown in combat was insufficient. Different versions of the aircraft, the MiG-17, were to be utilized by the 921st Fighter Regiment including the MiG-17 (sans suffix), the MiG-17F, both of which were built in the USSR, and the Shenyang F-5, which was built in the PRC, yet the type was considered obsolete by the Mikoyan-Gurevich design bureau that had created the aircraft, having been supplanted by the Mikoyan-Gurevich MiG-19 and the MiG-21.

Nonetheless, despite deficiencies in performance and armament in respect of the enemy aircraft to be encountered over the DRV, the MiG-17 could be an effective weapon. While incapable of flying beyond or at supersonic speed and unable to carry missiles, when flown by a capable pilot, the aircraft could gain advantage. Of particular note was the great manoeuvrability and powerful cannons of the robust MiG-17 which Nguyen Nhat Chieu surmised "was a good fighter that was dangerous at close quarters, [and] could accept very severe punishment and still bring the pilot back to base"[2].

The pilots were to concentrate on the development of tactics while gaining experience. The unit was governed by such practical limitations as which air bases were capable of supporting the aircraft and

---

[1] Ho Chi Minh quoted in Buza, Zoltán, Wings Of Fame, Volume 8, MiG-17 over Vietnam, p. 102.

[2] Nguyen Nhat Chieu quoted in Boniface, Roger, MiGs Over North Vietnam, p.138.

the consequent range of operations. It was decided that only when aerial strikes upon the DRV north of the 20th Parallel were made should the 921st Fighter Regiment be committed to combat.

Due to political concerns, particularly the possibility of intervention in the conflict by the PRC, the American units conducting the Rolling Thunder campaign were bound by variable conditions. Officially, the DRV and the USA were not at war and the government of the latter was confounded by the struggle with the government of the former which had the objective of unifying Vietnam. Initially, only targets located south of the 20th Parallel could be struck and even within that limitation approval from Secretary of Defense Robert McNamara and Johnson had to be given before a planned raid could be mounted.

Authorization was given to attack the bridges spanning the Song Ma River between 2 April and 8 April as Rolling Thunder program 9, the largest of which, the Thanh Hoa, was located at 19°50'17" north.

On 3 April four pilots of the 921st Fighter Regiment were placed on standby at 0500 hours and assigned a MiG-17 to respond to any aerial intrusion: Pham Ngoc Lan in 2310, Phan Van Tuc in 2118, Ho Van Quy in 2312, Tran Minh Phuong in 2318. Two others waited in reserve: Tran Hanh in 2316, Pham Giay in 2416. Radar detected a flight of aircraft which intruded and withdrew having, it seemed, conducted a reconnaissance. Observers spotted aircraft approaching the bridges over the Song Ma river at 0940 hours. Having been ordered into the air, the MiG-17s left the ground. At 1009 hours Pham Ngoc Lan reported the sighting of the offensive aircraft. The order was received to release drop tanks and attack!

Pham Ngoc Lan and Phan Van Tuc closed on two F-8s. Lan opened fire and one F-8 appeared to explode. Tuc sighted an F-8 then fired, apparently, causing the target to crash.

Ho Van Quy and Tran Minh Phuong pursued a pair of F-8s but were beyond range to gain hits.

The pilots were directed to land but Pham Ngoc Lan did not have enough fuel to reach Phuc Yen and, therefore, was ordered to eject. Determined to save the aircraft he searched for a site to make an approach. Both aircraft and pilot made a successful emergency landing along a bank of the Duong River and each was subsequently able to return to service.

There was jubilation amongst the 921st Fighter Regiment following the successful combat. Gun camera film was used to confirm the victories of Pham Ngoc Lan and Phan Van Tuc. 3 April has ever afterwards been celebrated as Vietnam People's Air Force Day.

It was believed that, having failed in the attempt to destroy the Thanh Hoa Bridge, the Americans would attack again so plans were made for an interception.

Indeed, American evaluation of the raid indicated but minor damage to the bridge and another assault was planned for the following day. A strike force of 48 Republic F-105 Thunderchiefs escorted by 10 North American F-100 Super Sabres was launched. Problems with refuelling and weather caused confusion and some F-105s were forced to orbit while awaiting a chance to attack the target.

Two flights of aircraft from the 921st Fighter Regiment were sent airborne, one at 0947 hours to attract attention, the other at 0948 hours to attack. Following the direction of ground control, contact was made with F-105s dropping bombs. Leading the attacking flight, Tran Hanh engaged and sent an F-105 down in flames and later related to Vietnamese media

> I shot at the nearest plane and hit its left wing. It staggered but tried to catch its formation. I sent another volley of bullets which hit the plane right in its body. It crashed to the ground, wrapped in black smoke and flame.[3]

A general melee ensued and Le Minh Huan was able to destroy a F-105. However, in the confusing clash, all four of the Vietnamese pilots engaged were forced down; three, Pham Giay, Le Minh Huan, Tran Nguyen Nam, being killed and Tran Hanh, flying MiG-17 2618, survived a landing, without using landing gear, in a field after running out of fuel. But one American pilot made a claim, Donald W. Kilgus flying a F-100, which was recognized as a probable victory, and it may be that Vietnamese pilots were killed in error by AAA fire.

No raids were mounted on the bridges over the Song Ma River on 5 April. With the respite one would imagine that the members of the 921st

---

[3] Tran Hanh quoted in O'Connor, Michael, Duel Over The Dragon's Jaw, AAHS Journal, American Aviation Historical Society, Volume 25 Number 4 Winter 1980, p.275.

Fighter Regiment were of mixed emotions. The interceptions were successful in destroying aircraft but the losses incurred in both men and machines were significant.

The response to and the results of the attacks were surprising to the Americans. Though intense and precise assaults, it was believed that the numerous aircraft were able to strike the span hundreds of times with missiles and bombs, the Thanh Hoa Bridge remained functional. What was more, losses, to all causes, were significant: one A-1, one A-4, one F-100 and three F-105s with four pilots killed and two pilots made prisoners of war and only one MiG-17 claimed probably destroyed in return.

Reconnaissance flights by the USAF and the USN on 5 April confirmed a development the Americans had anticipated; SAM sites were under construction in the environs of Hanoi. The skies over the DRV were defended by AAA and now aircraft as well. Soon the aggressors would attack in an environment made even more dangerous by the launching of guided missiles.

Conviction And Bravado

The command of the ADF-VPAF took measures, under the direction of advisors from the USSR, to integrate the detection of attacking aircraft and the weapons systems utilized in defence. Information garnered by radar and from observers was collected in regional command and control centres from which direction was given to the appropriate branch of aerial defence. AAA was to be used from low to medium altitudes and surface to air missiles were to be used from medium to high altitudes with aircraft operating at whatever altitude was deemed best within specific circumstances. While the destruction of attacking aircraft was paramount, the pilots could also be directed to other purposes such as drawing the enemy over anti aircraft weapons or missile systems or the interception of aircraft conducting missions of electronic surveillance or radar interference. The integration of the systems proved difficult and pilots were at risk of destruction by bullets, shells and missiles fired in error by comrades on the ground. Nonetheless, ground control of interceptions was a boon to the pilots of the VPAF who were given information about the location and direction of enemy aircraft as well as instruction as to where and when to attack.

The pilots of the 921st Fighter Regiment flying their silver swallows, as the MiG-17s were called, were much like others of the breed; proud, full of conviction and bravado, prone to exaggeration and resigned to casualties. Nonetheless, they were but few in number and they were inexperienced so, consequently, the unit suffered significant losses both in accidents and in combat. The leadership of both the DRV and the ADF-VPAF recognized that the American air forces, which committed a tremendous number of personnel and aircraft to the struggle, could not be defeated outright but that it was possible to disrupt operations and to inflict losses in material and men. The problems facing the airmen were recognized and acknowledged. With mature consideration those in command sought to commit the MiG-17s only when at an advantage. Much remained to be done to make the defence forces effective.

Combats occurred through the summer and casualties were suffered. During a battle on 17 June, with USN aircraft of the USS Midway, two McDonnell Douglas F-4 Phantom IIs were claimed sent down but three MiG-17s were destroyed; Cao Thanh Tinh and Nguyen Nhat Chieu were both forced to eject and the MiG-17 of Le Trong Long, who was credited with the destruction of a F-4, was flown into a mountain. In the course of a scrap with A-1s, at low altitude, on 20 June, in which two were thought to have been shot down, a MiG-17 crashed and Nguyen Van Lai was killed. A struggle on 10 July, with F-4s of the USAF, resulted in the death of Phan Thanh Nha and Nguyen Cuong. Such losses of aircraft and pilots were of great consequence to a force with such limited resources. With only few pilots and aircraft available for operations, the unit was directed to avoid combat.

Nonetheless, the struggle continued as strikes were made by the American air forces upon the transportation networks of the DRV. On 20 September the weather conditions seemed to preclude flight operations but pilots, who had been told to stand down, were suddenly ordered to return to active duty to face an attack by the enemy along Route 1 between Hanoi and Lang Son. Abandoning a meal being eaten, they rushed to Phuc Yen; Nguyen Ngoc Do, Nguyen Nhat Chieu, Tran Van Tri and Pham Ngoc Lan, who led the flight, receiving orders only after taking to the air. Aircraft were seen over Yen Tu and identified as F-4s of the USN. Chieu was to remember "I latched onto a F-4 and fired a short burst but missed ... I then closed in and fired again and observed hits so I closed in even further and fired until I ran out of ammunition"[4]. The target was seen to burn and crash which was confirmed by Lan, who saw the aircraft strike a mountain, before leading the pilots back, safely, to Phuc Yen.

The final victory of year was claimed on 6 November by a pilot of the 921st Fighter Regiment, Ngo Doan Nhung, over a Sikorsky CH-3 Jolly Green Giant attempting a search and rescue (SAR) mission to recover an American pilot downed previously by a SAM.

Hill Of The Peaceful Site

In May, following the entry of the 921st Fighter Regiment into combat, the government of the DRV had called for the creation of a new airbase, Kep, to be completed by September. Tremendous effort was required utilizing workers from the Bac Giang chemical fertilizer plant and the 305th Division of the VPA. Explosives needed to be used to reconfigure the landscape and a river had to be diverted to a canal, but, the facility, complete with taxiways and runways as well as service roads, was opened for use on 7 September which was the same day that the 923rd Hill Of The Peaceful Site Fighter Regiment was established under the command of Nguyen Phuc Trach.

Kep presented difficulties to the pilots of the 923rd Fighter Regiment. The geography of the area, with hills in the environs, made landing the MiG-17 difficult. Training was undertaken at Phuc Yen with the dimensions of the runway at Kep marked, where the runway was of lesser length, and, initially, pilots could not bring a MiG-17 to a halt within the confines indicated. The limited amount of aircraft shelters meant that, temporarily, only four of the 923rd Fighter Regiment's aircraft could be kept at Kep with the remainder being based at Phuc Yen. Pilots were rotated to the PRC for additional training. Yet, less than a month after formation, MiG-17s of the 923rd Fighter Regiment were in combat.

---

[4] Nguyen Nhat Chieu quoted in Boniface, Roger, <u>MiGs Over North Vietnam</u>, p.139

On 6 October, four MiG-17s, under the leadership of Tran Huyen, intercepted a formation of USN F-4s. While trying to manoeuvre behind one of the F-4s, Nguyen Van Bay saw a missile launched and successfully turned in avoidance but the consequent explosion of the warhead in proximity sent the MiG-17 out of control. Regaining mastery while flying at speed, a piece of shrapnel was noticed lodged in the canopy. "I put my hand over the hole but felt it being sucked out. "Oh, it's Bernoulli's Law", I thought to myself"[5]. Further reflection on the laws of aerodynamics was not possible, however, as the MiG-17 had suffered extensive damage necessitating that Bay make an emergency landing at Phuc Yen after which some 82 holes were counted in the aircraft.

Consolidated

New aircraft, MiG-17PFs as well as MiG-21PFLs were delivered from the USSR as were P-35 and PRV-11 radar systems, the former to detect at range, the latter to detect at altitude, to improve the defensive capabilities of the ADF-VPAF. The 921st Fighter regiment was to operate both the MiG-17 and the MiG-21 while the 923rd Fighter regiment was equipped with the MiG-17 and the Shenyang JJ-2, the version of the Mikoyan-Gurevich MiG-15UTI built in the PRC, for training purposes. Other airbases had been and were being developed so as to be able to operate jet aircraft so, in combination with Phuc Yen, to the northwest of Hanoi and Kep to the northeast of Hanoi, the VPAF would have available a network of sites from which to plan operations and respond to developing situations.

The MiG-21 would allow the VPAF the possibility to interfere with all aspects of American aerial attack being capable of both attaining supersonic flight and carrying missile armament, however, great skill was necessary to utilize the aircraft to maximum advantage and pilots required training at length which was done, both, in the USSR and in the DRV. The physical demands of flight beyond the speed of sound proved a great problem for the Vietnamese pilots small of stature and slight of

---

[5] Nguyen Van Bay quoted in Toperczer, István, MiG-17/19 Aces Of The Vietnam War, p.23.

build. As well as mastering the flying of the aircraft, pilots had to learn how to use the different weapons systems which versions of the MiG-21 were capable of mounting including cannon and a variety of air to air missiles (AAM) including the RS-2US, the S-5 and, the R-3S which was heat seeking and the optimal armament.

With a greater amount of AAA in service, due to the enlargement of the militia, and the availability of the S-75 Dvina SAM, with which a first victory, a F-4, was claimed on 24 July, in increasing numbers in addition to, now, two Fighter Regiments, the three basic defensive systems of the ADV-VPAF had not only been established but consolidated.

Between the final days of 1965 and the first days of 1966 the VPAF became involved in but few combats due to a concentration on training. A temporary halt to Rolling Thunder operations while negotiations were undertaken with the DRV and seasonal storms limited aerial operations by the American air forces. Still, there were actions of significance. On 3 February 1966 the first claims by a pilot trained to attack aircraft at night, Lam Van Lich, flying radar equipped MiG-17PF 4721, were made, two A-1s shot down in darkness, in the vicinity of Mai Chau. On 4 March Nguyen Hong Nhi destroyed a reconnaissance drone to the north of Hanoi flying a MiG-21F-13 and thereby became the first pilot to claim a victory while utilizing the type with the VPAF.

To Be Tested Anew

Frustrated by the continual support given the NLFSV by the DRV, which precluded a peaceful settlement to the conflict with the USA, but enabled by the advent of weather favourable for aerial operations, American air forces were authorized to range across the DRV with the exception of the exclusion zone along the border with the PRC and populated areas designated within Haiphong and Hanoi. Railway yards and power plants were struck and the list of potential targets was enlarged to include oil storage sites. With more sorties against more objectives authorized, the USAF and the USN agreed, formally, to divide the DRV into six areas known as Route Packages and assign each air force the responsibility to undertake missions over specific areas. The USAF, based in The Kingdom of Thailand (KT) and the RVN, was assigned Route

Packages I, V and VIa, which included Hanoi while the USN, stationed in the Gulf of Tonkin, was assigned Route Packages, II, III, IV and VIb, which included Haiphong. Flying regular routes in designated regions allowed airmen to become familiar with weather patterns, terrain and the defences to be faced when attacking which made possible the effective planning of operations. The defences of the DRV against aerial attack were to be tested anew and no element more so than the VPAF.

Sustained Activity

While the pilots of the 921st Fighter Regiment struggled to utilize the MiG-21 effectively, on 4 March Ngo Duc Mai fired on a F-4 to record the initial claim of the 923rd Fighter Regiment, thus, beginning a period of sustained activity for the unit. Flying the MiG-17, an aircraft of inferior capabilities, to deal with a, potentially, overwhelming force, the optimum choice was to utilize hit and run tactics which required precise ground control so as to bring the pilot within the range of the cannon armament while allowing for disengagement when necessary. Rising from below a formation and directed to attack specific aircraft, pilots had a chance to claim a victory if unseen for as Luu Huy Chao related "when the American pilots saw us they just flew away in a flash"[6]. If engaged in combat and forced to defend, however, it was realized that when flying the MiG-17 advantage could be gained over an enemy piloting powerful aircraft at low altitude in horizontal flight at low speed, yet, once engaged it was not always possible to dictate terms.   Such considerations made the destruction of enemy aircraft difficult.   Nonetheless, pilots of the 923rd Fighter Regiment were able to claim victories in combat with aircraft of both the USAF and the USN.

On 29 June simultaneous strikes were made on fuel storage sites by the USN, at Thuong Ly near Haiphong, and by the USAF, at Duc Giang near Hanoi.   Four MiG-17s of the 923rd Fighter Regiment, flown as two pairs, Tran Huyen with Vo Van Man and Nguyen Van Bay with Phan Van Tuc took off from Phuc Yen. The Vietnamese pilots spotted four F-105s from

---

[6] Luu Huy Chao quoted in Appy, Christian G., ed., Patriots The Vietnam War Remembered From All Sides, p.214.

which the bombs carried were dropped as the American pilots prepared to defend themselves.   The pairs each battled a brace of the enemy.   The pilots of the F-105s attempted to turn on the MiG-17s but as the aircraft manoeuvred the speed of the combat slowed.   The advantage was to the pilots of the MiG-17s as Huyen claimed to have damaged one F-105 while Bay set one afire following which Tuc claimed another destroyed.   The pilots of the F-105s fled as possible.   Warned by ground control of the presence of American aircraft in the vicinity of Phuc Yen, the airmen of the 923rd Fighter Regiment were directed to the Gia Lam airbase, originally built in 1932 to administer to the needs of French civil aviation in the area of Hanoi, which had been made capable of sustaining the military aircraft operated by the VPAF, where all four made successful landings.   After analysis of the combat had been completed, Nguyen Van Bay and Phan Van Tuc were given credit for the shared destruction of two F-105s. Actually, one F-105 was destroyed, from which Murphy N. Jones was made a prisoner of war, and three other F-105s were damaged, nonetheless, by forcing the abandonment of ordnance and causing the destruction and damaging of aircraft at no cost the interception was a success.

Pilots flying the MiG-21, however, had been frustrated by the complexities of capability and aircraft were lost due to both error and combat.   On 26 April two MiG-21s had taken off from Phuc Yen to intercept a Douglas EB-66 Destroyer but were set upon by escorting F-4s; Dong Van Song turned away and three missiles were fired at Nguyen Hong Nhi who ejected from the aircraft which was damaged by the first missile and destroyed by the third. Being the first crew of the USAF to down a MiG-21, upon landing, aircraft commander Paul J. Gilmore and pilot William T. Smith may well have been given slaps on the back but the unfortunate Nhi sustained back injury.

Limited both by armament and command from the ground, pilots were unable to utilize the MiG-21 to potential; combat seldom resulted in success. Neither the RS-2US or S-5 missiles, which lacked guidance, proved effective against a maneuvering aircraft but the R-3S missile which was capable of destroying an evading aircraft was not available in quantity. The application of ground controlled interception (GCI) without the appreciation of flexibility resulted in attacks by a pair of aircraft flown in close proximity by pilots left unable to respond to a developing situation.

With experience gained it was determined that a GCI was best made by a pair of aircraft directed to fly some distance apart at the highest possible speed from the rear of an attacking formation. The pilot of the leading aircraft which was armed with R-3S missiles would attack while the pilot of the supporting aircraft would watch for any threat by an enemy. Both would attempt to leave the scene without further engagement to, if warranted, be directed to another attack by the command tracking the situation.

Two EB-66s, escorted by four F-4s were airborne providing electronic support of a strike on a bridge to the southwest of Yen Bai on 5 October. One of the escorts was suddenly seen aflame by the crew of another escort though no enemy was in sight.   Aircraft commander Edward W. Garland and pilot William R. Andrews ejected and a SAR operation, in which two helicopters were damaged by fire from the ground, was mounted rescuing the former while the latter, having been wounded, was not found and was subsequently confirmed as dead. The aircraft had been intercepted by an element of the 921st Fighter Regiment; MiG-21s flown by Bui Dinh Kinh and Nguyen Dang Kinh.   Directed by ground control, approaching from altitude at speed, the two pilots conducted a precise attack. While Nguyen Dang Kinh watched for any threat Bui Dinh Kinh fired an R-3S missile which struck the target and then the MiG-21s were able to egress without having been spotted.

A recent development had made the aggressive use of the limited resources of the VPAF all the more necessary. Electronic counter measure (ECM) pods carried on strike aircraft had been introduced by the USAF in the autumn in an effort to limit the effectiveness of the SAMs and radar directed AAA employed by the ADF-VPAF and, while the threats were never eliminated, ECM technology was applied with immediate success and casualties were reduced to a significant degree. It, therefore, became all the more important that the pilots of the MiG-17s and MiG-21s engage effectively.

At Disadvantage

Contentious use of the MiG-21s of the 921st Fighter Regiment, particularly in the defence of the region surrounding Hanoi, resulted in quantities of ordnance dropped other than on target and aircraft lost by the USAF, especially on strikes within Route Package VIa. For fear of killing advisors from the countries offering support to the VPAF, attacks upon airfields in the DRV were not permitted, so increasing the effectiveness of strikes and reducing the casualties endured would have to come as a result of aerial combat. Extensive planning was undertaken in the 8th Tactical Fighter Wing (TFW) to induce the pilots of the 921st Fighter Regiment into a situation at disadvantage.

Just such a scenario, was played out on 2 January 1967 under the moniker of Operation Bolo. Ground control released two flights of four MiG-21s sequentially when F-4s were in the vicinity of Phuc Yen. The MiG-21s emerged from cloud cover, one after the other, to be set upon. Each of the first flight was destroyed as was the first of the second flight. Five MiG-21s were shot down but, the pilots, Bui Duc Nhu, Nguyen Dang Kinh, Nguyen Duc Thuan, Vu Ngoc Dinh, of the first flight and Nguyen Ngoc Do, of the second flight, were each fortunate to be able to eject. Nguyen Van Coc, having flown with the second flight was later to comment "This serious loss was due to the late take-off of the alert aircraft, indecisiveness in the Central Command Post and a faulty concept; we expected F-105s"[7].

In the following days further attempts were made to intercept USAF aircraft, though, without success. Flawed ground control, apparently unaware of all of the F-4s within the range of an attempted attack, resulted in the loss of two MiG-21s, one flown by Dong Van De, who was killed, and one flown by Mai Van Cuong, who was able to eject, on 6 January. The 921st Fighter Regiment was left with but few serviceable aircraft and would be able to mount but few sorties. On 8 January command of the VPAF instigated a conference to review the situation and determine how to respond following the significant losses endured. It was concluded that the aircraft attacking should change speed and altitude while approaching targets and, following recommendations made by advisors from the USSR, it was decided that interceptions should be conducted against enemy aircraft after having assumed a formation and away from Phuc Yen. It was recognized that ground control needed to be

---

[7] Nguyen Van Coc quoted in Davies, Peter, F-4 Phantom II Vs MiG-21, p.56.

administered with lessened constraint and the observations of pilots had to be taken into consideration when decisions were made.

While the 921st Fighter Regiment struggled to develop effective ground control doctrine, the 923rd Fighter Regiment remained active and efficient when able to respond to attacks. A strike on rail targets at Dap Cau on 16 September 1966 was intercepted by a flight of MiG-17s from which Nguyen Van Bay made a claim. The F-4 destroyed was recognized by the VPAF as the fifth victory of Bay who, thus, became the first Vietnamese pilot to be acknowledged as an ace and was much celebrated by media in the DRV and even invited to dine with Ho Chi Minh.

Inclement weather impeded aerial operations with the result that interceptions were few, but the transfer of the 923rd Fighter Regiment from Kep to Gia Lam was undertaken. On 24 March 1967 administrative changes were made to the ADF-VPAF that included the formation of 371st Thang Long Air Division which integrated the command structure of the existing Fighter Regiments, the 921st and 923rd, as well as the 919th Air Transport Regiment. Though the VPAF remained limited in both human and material resources, decisions were made to return the 921st Fighter Regiment to the fray in earnest with the 923rd Fighter Regiment which, once the weather improved, together with the other forces of the ADF-VPAF, would mount a sustained effort to defend the DRV.

Decisions had also been made elsewhere. An increase in strike activity by the American air forces had been planned. Authorization was given as necessary by the appropriate elements of the American government which also allowed a further expansion of objectives to be attacked including sites of economic significance, such as the Thai Nguyen Steel Mill, and of military importance which included airbases being used by the Fighter Regiments of the VPAF.

Undeterred

On 19 April four F-105s flying an Iron Hand flight meant to suppress AAA sites and SAM sites, in support of an attack on a VPA base at Xuan Mai, were attacked by a group of MiG-17s. One of the American aircraft was shot down, two were damaged and left the area while one remained in the vicinity as pilot Leo K. Thorsness and electronic warfare officer (EWO) Harold E. Johnson, an experienced and resourceful crew who together had devised methods by which to attack SAM sites, sought to assist the SAR mission instigated to retrieve pilot Thomas M. Madison and EWO Thomas J. Sterling. Two A-1s arrived to participate in the recovery operation but several MiG-17s attacked. One A-1 was hit by cannon rounds and crashed and the pilot, John S. Hamilton, was killed. Thorsness and Johnson, having flown away, returned and entered the combat as did another flight of F-105s while the other A-1 escaped following which the air battle ended. With two aircraft destroyed, two aircraft damaged and one pilot killed and a pilot and a EWO captured, the mission had proved a difficult one for the USAF and, while four MiG-17s were claimed destroyed, in fact, none were lost. Indeed, the 923rd Fighter Regiment, flying from Gia Lam, had been in combat, but, no losses were recorded while two F-105s and two A-1s were claimed destroyed. Apparently, Nguyen Ba Dich downed the F-105 of Madison and Sterling and Nguyen Van Tho downed the A-1 of Hamilton but the other two aircraft, claimed by Duong Trung Tan, were able to leave the battle and land safely. Fighter pilots, no mater nationality, are, generally, of the optimistic sort.

In addition to Gia Lam, the 923rd Fighter Regiment began to sortie from the airbases of Hoa Lac, west of Hanoi and Kien An south of Haiphong. Numerous interceptions were flown in April and several victories were claimed against both the USAF and the USN which began to attack the facilities of the VPAF as a means of reducing losses. It became a necessary act of preservation to both camouflage and move the MiG-17s and MiG-21s, a task often fulfilled by the mighty Mil Mi-6 which could lift and transport an aircraft to sanctuary of a sort.

Nguyen Van Bay made what was to be a final claim on 29 April; a F-4 shot down some distance west of Hanoi was confirmed as the seventh victory of the ace. It was decided that the life of a pilot who had accumulated such experience and was of such popularity could no longer be risked in combat. A sortie was made on May Day, but afterwards, though continuing to serve with the 923rd Fighter Regiment as a Command Duty Officer, Bay was no longer permitted to fly on operations.

MiG-21s of the 921st Fighter Regiment were in combat in the hope that improvements made to ground control procedures would not only reduce casualties but enhance capability. On 23 April Nguyen Dang Kinh was shot down flying a MiG-21, being fortunate to eject and survive, for a third time at that, and on 26 April Tran Thien Luong was shot down flying a MiG-21 but, ejecting at low altitude, was killed when impacting with the earth.   Undeterred, on 28 April, the 921st Fighter Regiment sent two MiG-21s aloft to intercept aircraft following a strike on locomotive repair facilities in Hanoi and, indeed, F-105s were attacked by Dang Ngoc Ngu and Mai Van Cong who destroyed one of the enemy.   30 April was to be a day of intense aerial activity over the DRV as the USAF launched an attack on the energy production infrastructure in Hanoi which resulted in a response from the 921st Fighter Regiment.   Two flights of two, Nguyen Ngoc Do with Nguyen Van Coc and Le Trong Huyen with Vu Ngoc Dinh, took off to be directed precisely by ground control.   Above and behind F-105s en route to Vinh Phu the pilots of the MiG-21s dove to the attack. Nguyen Ngoc Do then Nguyen Van Coc destroyed a F-105 following which both were ordered to return and land.   Bombers on the strike dropped ordnance and other F-105s were beset by by Le Trong Huyen and Vu Ngoc Dinh each of whom claimed one destroyed before returning to safely. Both the MiG-21 and the R-3S missile had proved effective as three F-105s were destroyed, one other was damaged and four airmen were made prisoners of war, Joseph S. Abbott, Robert A. Abbott and the crew of Leo K. Thorsness and Harold E. Johnson who had so recently flown with great courage during the combat with MiG-17s of the 923rd Fighter Regiment on 19 April.

Success resulted in an acknowledgement of the effectiveness of the VPAF by the USAF.   F-4s had performed as bombers prepared to become fighters carrying a payload that was to be dropped if MiG-17s or MiG-21s attacked to permit greater maneuverability.   In an attempt to reduce losses, the decision was made that such aircraft should no longer carry bombs at all, but act as escorts so as to supplement the F-4s which had been assigned the task of protecting bombers and such a provision was also applied to some F-105s; aircraft which could have been dropping bombs on the DRV were being forced to give up offence to provide defence.

However, the increased number of escorts as well as the introduction of an enhanced location and identification system and the adaptation of cannon armament by F-4s meant that the Vietnamese pilots were under greater threat from the enemy than ever before.

The air forces engaged entered into many combats of complexity and confusion and made several claims, some of which, but by no means all of, can be substantiated. Even pilots of capability and experience found the skies over the DRV challenging in the extreme. On 4 May, Nguyen Van Coc, able to fly both the MiG-17 and the MiG-21 and with an initial victory claimed and confirmed, was intent on pursuing and destroying a F-105, but was shot down by aircraft commander Robin Olds and pilot William D. Lefever, who fired several missiles at the MiG-21 wildly manoeuvring through the air, though was able to eject safely over Phuc Yen "when at an altitude of 100 metres ... with speed of 260 kilometres an hour" and saw the aircraft flown crash "at a distance of 500 metres from the runway"[8]. Olds may well have been the most experienced airman in theatre, having flown on operations in the Second World War and amassing 13 victories during the conflict, but pilot Norman C. Gaddis too had aerial experience dating back to the Second World War and had left the Fighter Weapons School to serve in the KT as the commander of the 12th TFW. No matter the skills acquired, when flying with Weapons Systems Operator (WSO) James M. Jefferson, on 12 May Gaddis was shot down, apparently, by Ngo Duc Mai flying a MiG-17, and though Jefferson was killed, Gaddis survived to become a prisoner of war. However, subsequent to such success, the 923rd Fighter Regiment was to suffer demoralizing losses; Nguyen The Hon and Vo Van Man, each having claimed aircraft destroyed, were shot down and killed in combat with F-4s on 14 May.

While the American air forces were well able to deal with attrition such was not true of the VPAF. Several aircraft were lost both to attacks on the ground and in the air. Faced with numerous escorts protecting the bombers, pilots had to take great care to avoid being shot down. Those flying the MiG-17 were forced to apply defensive tactics. When attacked, flights flew in formation, turning in a continuous circle whereby the pilot behind could protect the pilot ahead; doing so limited losses but also limited the opportunities for downing the aircraft of the enemy. Those flying the MiG-21 relied on ground control to enable an attack. Only when

---

[8] Nguyen Van Coc quoted in Toperczer, Istvan, MiG Aces of the Vietnam War, p.78.

accurately directed to the enemy was success achievable. Combat was intense and though claims were made, so too, were losses suffered, losses in numbers that the VPAF could not endure without consequence. Hoang Van Ky, who had flown with both the 921st Fighter Regiment and the 923rd Fighter Regiment and been credited with several victories, was killed in action with F-4s on 5 June as were fellow MiG-17 pilots Tran Huyen and Truong Van Cung.

With limited numbers of both men and machines, Van Tien Dung, Chief of the General Staff of the VPA, had to order the preservation of resources as there were but few experienced pilots and operational aircraft remaining. The restoration of damaged and worn MiG-17s and MiG-21s to serviceability as well as the recuperation of exhausted pilots meant that sorties were limited, consequently, there were few combats and, thus, few claims for some time. In respect of future operations, new tactics discussed were to be applied, but such was the shortage of aircraft, that training exercises had to be conducted with the same aircraft which would otherwise be used in combat.

The American air forces were able to launch strikes upon the DRV without particular concern for interception. F-4s that had been designated to protect bombers were, as previously, directed to carry ordnance. It was considered that the VPAF had been defeated and William A. Momyer, the overall administrator of the USAF operations in theatre, said as much to the Senate Subcommittee on Defense Preparedness on 12 August.

Better Attack Position

On 23 August a pair of MiG-21s of the 921st Fighter Regiment were sent aloft from Phuc Yen to intercept a raid on the Yen Vien rail yards by the USAF. Pilots Nguyen Nhat Chieu and Nguyen Van Coc flew towards the aircraft, parallel on one flank, at low altitude so as to remain unseen by airborne radar systems and, when aside the formation and beyond the range of aerial detection, were directed by ground control to climb above cloud cover then, when over and behind the enemy, to dive through the overcast accelerating and fire R-3S missiles at targets. Flying as directed, both Chieu and Coc destroyed a F-4 then made a second attack, though, without being able to claim further victories and, in fact, the former fired cannon shells at the latter in a moment of confusion causing some damage but both were able to land successfully.

Nguyen Van Coc described the action succinctly; "The leader Nguyen Nhat Chieu and I went the long way around to get into a better attack position from the back"[9].

MiG-17s of the 923rd Fighter Regiment also took to the air. Cao Thanh Tinh claimed a victory as did Le Hong Diep and Nguyen Van Tho though Le Van Phong was killed in action. The strike had proved arduous for the USAF; four F-4s were lost in total and aircrew casualties incurred included two killed, two wounded and four made prisoners of war.

Telling was the fact that subsequently, as before, particular F-4s that had been carrying ordnance were designated to fly without bombs as escorts.

September was a month of intense aerial combat and though no claims were made by the American air forces several were made by the VPAF. Reconnaissance aircraft were targeted by the 921st Fighter Regiment and Nguyen Hong Nhi claimed a McDonnell RF-101 Voodoo on 10 September and on 16 September, flying MiG-21 F-13s recently supplied by the Republic of Cuba (RC), Nguyen Ngoc Do and Pham Thanh Ngan were each acknowledged as downing a RF-101 sent to photograph rail lines in the northwest of the DRV as well; actions which discouraged the USAF from mounting further such operations with the type. Of particular significance, however, was the fact that through the month forty seven aircraft on strike missions dropped the ordnance carried in order to escape from attacking MiG-17s and MiG-21s. Such success was to continue for on 2 October 16 aircraft had to drop bomb loads other than over the intended target when beset by aircraft of the VPAF. Several victories were claimed by Vietnamese pilots in the first days of the month including a F-105 each by the formidable pair of Nguyen Nhat Chieu and Nguyen Van Coc on 7 October and another F-105 by Nguyen Hong Nhi on 9 October. Clearly, the VPAF had not been defeated.

---

[9] Nguyen Van Coc quoted in Toperczer, István, Silver Swallows And Blue Bandits, p. 107.

Proficiency And Confidence

Strikes had been made upon every major airbase administered by the ADF-VPAF bar one and that one was of the greatest importance to the Vietnamese because of the facilities on hand and the proximity to Hanoi. The apparent resurgence of VPAF convinced the government of the USA that attacks on Phuc Yen had to be authorized no matter the concerns for foreign advisors in the vicinity. Within the American air forces, many were the aircrew eager to take part in the strikes upon a target, previously forbidden from assault, so significant both in the material and the abstract.

Phuc Yen was bombed on two consecutive days, 24 and 25 October and the Americans insisted much damage was done. It was believed that some 12 aircraft were destroyed. Other targets, elements of the infrastructure of the DRV, were bombed as well, including the Long Bien Bridge which spanned the Red River and served as means of transporting goods to Hanoi which had been delivered to Haiphong.

The Fighter Regiments interfered, but, the dispersal of aircraft was made necessary by the attacks on airbases and, consequently, coordinating interceptions was made difficult and only two victories were claimed, on 25 October, a F-105 by Nguyen Huu Tao and a F-4 by Nguyen Phu Ninh, both of whom flew the MiG-17 with the 923rd Fighter Regiment. Several aircraft were lost, though, including MiG-21s of the 921st Fighter Regiment flown by Dong Van Song on 24 October, who ejected for a third time, and Mai Van Cuong on 26 October, who ejected for a second time. The 923rd Fighter Regiment also suffered losses on 26 October when three pilots were forced to eject, Le Si Diep and Nguyen Hong Thai enduring a unique experience while Duong Trung Tan was given a second opportunity to appreciate the cartridge fired ejection seat installed in the MiG-17.

Despite the damage to airbases, the losses of material and inclement weather, the VPAF continued to rise to the defence of the DRV. The successive strikes by the American air forces prompted a decision to have a brace of aircraft ready to intercept throughout the day. On 7 November Nguyen Dang Kinh and Nguyen Hong Nhi of the 921st Fighter Regiment were flown by Mil Mi-4 from Gia Lam to Phuc Yen and there waited on stand by until ordered into the air to intercept a strike, apparently headed for Hanoi, and the latter claimed a F-105 and the former claimed a F-4 before both, running short of fuel, had to make emergency, but, successful landings. The very next day another encounter resulted in the destruction of a F-4 engaged on a combat air patrol (CAP) mission by Dang Ngoc Ngu while flying a MiG-21 with the 921st Fighter Regiment.   Further successful combats by the unit followed causing enemy aircraft to drop the payload carried while several pilots were awarded confirmation of victories including Pham Thanh Ngan and Nguyen Van Coc who each claimed a F-105 destroyed on 18 November, a feat the two pilots repeated on 20 November. The Fighter Regiments and the Missile Regiments incurred such significant losses upon the USAF and the USN as to prompt a conference at the Pacific Air Forces headquarters which set the goal of reducing casualties.

Though storms impeded aerial operations, strikes were mounted when possible and both the tactics used and the skills applied by the ADF-VPAF to counter the efforts of the foe continued to meet with success. Advice from foreign advisors and experience garnered enabled ground control to develop the capacity to simultaneously direct multiple pairs effectively, even of different types, thereby allowing the tactical integration of the MiG-17 and the MiG-21 in the air. GCIs were regularly conducted successfully.

The ever increasing proficiency and confidence of the VPAF pilots enabled multiple attacks on a mission and even when unable to penetrate defensive formations those flying the MiG-21 would fire R-3S missiles causing aircrew to drop ordnance in order to undertake evasive manoeuvres. The intent of ground control was to direct one MiG-21 to a position far behind and above enemy aircraft then attack causing dispersal and destruction following which another MiG-21 would attack in the same manner. American pilots found the situation frustrating.

Four F-4s of the CAP of a strike on 16 December, flying in pairs, engaged a formation of MiG-17s flying in a continuous circle over Kep but neither force could gain advantage. One pair gave up the fight while the other pair continued the struggle until forced to retire due to a lack of fuel. A MiG-21 directed towards the F-4s, which were flying at a low speed to conserve kerosene, fired an R-3S missile which struck one. The crew of aircraft commander James F. Low and pilot Howard J. Hill ejected to become prisoners of war.

Low was an experienced airman having flown with the 335th Fighter Interceptor Squadron of the 4th Fighter Interceptor Group during the war in Korea and becoming the junior American ace of the conflict being credited with a fifth victory six months after being rated a pilot. He was deemed to have downed a total of nine Mikoyan-Gurevich MiG-15s, received numerous decorations and be featured as a character in the novel The Hunters by James Salter. Low was surprised by the negligence that governed the mission but what would have been more surprising, had the fact been known at the time, was that the pilot who shot down USAF F-4D 66-7631 was from the Democratic People's Republic of Korea (DPRK)!

Group Z

Some American aircrew believed that MiG-17s and MiG-21s that rose in the defence of the DRV were flown, not only by Vietnamese, but by pilots from other countries as well. Instructors from the USSR and other socialist nations did train and advise members of the VPAF in the DRV, but the only country from which pilots came to serve in combat was the DPRK. Following the concluding of an agreement between military staff of the two nations in 1966, which was personally overseen by Vo Nguyen Giap, one unit flying the MiG-21F-13, with the 921st Fighter Regiment, and two units flying the Shenyang J-5 version of the MiG-17 with the 923rd Fighter Regiment, both versions of the aircraft with which the Koreans were familiar, were formed under the command of Kim Chang Xon with the designation Group Z. While the members of the units were staffed by and led by Koreans, Vietnamese of the ADF-VPAF provided the uniforms worn, the aircraft flown and assigned missions.

Group Z became operational in February 1967. Kim Quang Wook, flying a Shenyang J-5, was the first casualty, being shot down by Max C. Brestal piloting a F-105 on 10 March. A claim for an initial victory by a Korean pilot attached to the 923rd Fighter Regiment, flying a Shenyang J-5 in combat with F-4s, was made on 24 April while on 30 May one of a group of A-4s was the first victory credited to a Korean pilot flying a MiG-21 with the 921st Fighter Regiment. Ernest contributions to the defence of the

DRV by Group Z continued until 1969 by which time the Koreans, believed to have numbered 87 in total, had claimed 26 victories at the cost of 14 pilots killed though VPAF records acknowledge 12 aircraft lost and eight victories credited.

Aggressive Intent

Rather than responding exclusively to American excursions into the DRV in a defensive manner the VPAF began to sortie aircraft with aggressive intent, claiming three F-105s and a F-4 destroyed on 3 January 1968 for the loss of a MiG-17 from which Le Hong Diep was able to eject. Flying from Phuc Yen in MiG-21s of the 921st Fighter Regiment, Dong Van Song and Nguyen Dang Kinh set off to intercept an EB-66 engaging on an electronic support mission on 14 January.   Attacking the target mid afternoon, Kinh fired two missiles which missed but Song closed and the R-3S missile launched struck the starboard engine causing the EB-66 to crash. MiG-21s were sent off in larger formations, a pair in the company of another, a pair of pairs, and flown south of potential targets in an effort to force enemy aircraft to drop ordnance.   The monsoon limited the opportunities for combat but the engagements that did occur were fought vigorously as on 3 February when two Convair F-102 Delta Daggers participating in a CAP were attacked by pilots of the 921st Fighter Regiment near the border between the DRV and the KL. Several missiles were fired by both the Vietnamese and the Americans, of which one lodged in the tail of the aircraft flown by Wallace L. Wiggins who was killed when another, apparently fired by MiG-21 pilot Pham Thanh Ngan, caused a comprehensive explosion.

The very success of the Vietnamese pilots in the air meant that Vietnamese aircraft would be attacked on the ground. Phuc Yen, was the target of a strike on 14 February by four aircraft bombing escorted by two flights of F-4s and two flights of F-105s. Two MiG-17s were claimed destroyed in combat and one, flown by 923rd Fighter Regiment pilot Nguyen Chiem, who ejected, was.

On February 23 Hoang Bieu, flying a MiG-21 with the 921st Fighter Regiment, took off from Phuc Yen and intercepted a CAP flight in the company of two pilots of Group Z.   The Vietnamese and one of the

Koreans claimed a hit on the same F-4. Pilot Laird Gutterson and WSO Myron L. Donald were forced to eject to become prisoners of war.

Events Previously Unimaginable

However effective the efforts of the VPAF were, for the people of the DRV beneath the falling bombs, Rolling Thunder was as a force of nature: unstoppable. Yet events previously unimaginable were to bring an end to the aerial campaign. With the new year on 30 January had come the Tet Offensive launched by the NLFSV and on 31 March Johnson announced there would be no attempt to retain the office of the President.

The NLFSV attempted to instigate a popular uprising throughout the RVN by staging simultaneous attacks against both RVN and American forces. While an effort surprising and spectacular, the offensive was crushed by military forces before political cadres were able to mobilize the population and an outright revolution was prevented. Yet, though ultimately a failure, the Tet Offensive was an event of such shock and magnitude as to cause a reassessment of American policy by the public and the government of the nation.

After consultation and deliberation, on 31 March Johnson announced that aircraft would make no attacks on the DRV far beyond the area of the Demilitarized Zone which divided the north and the south as part of an effort to reduce violence prior to declaring that the nomination of the Democratic Party for the office of the President would neither be sought or accepted.

While strikes continued to be launched against the DRV, the targets were to be south of the 20th Parallel and eventually all missions to be conducted were within Route Package I, assigned to the USAF, Route Package II and Route Package III, both of which were assigned to the USN. In order to engage the attacking aircraft it was necessary to send elements south. MiG-17s of the 923rd Fighter Regiment were sent to the Vinh airbase in April and MiG-21s of the 921st Fighter Regiment were sent to the Tho Xuan airbase in May.

The task of intercepting aircraft was made difficult for the ADF-VPAF by a lack of GCI infrastructure in the area and the presence of SAMs, in the form of RIM-8 Talos missiles, on board USN vessels in the Gulf Of Tonkin. Problems were encountered on 7 May when MiG-21s sent aloft came under the fire of Vietnamese AAA and then one pair of fighters was almost led to attack another pair of fighters. Despite confusion and frustration Nguyen Van Coc was able to destroy an F-4 with an R-3S missile.

USN aircraft which struck airbases in the area were able to reach sanctuary over the fleet off the coast. Flying too close put VPAF aircraft in peril to SAMs launched from ships. Ha Quang Hung, on 23 May, and Nguyen Van Ly and Vu Dinh Rang, on 22 September, of the 921st Fighter Regiment, were all fortunate to eject safely after the MiG-21s flown were damaged by Talos missiles.

Between the losses, on 16 June, however, Dinh Ton despatched a F-4 flying to the coast, without coming under SAM fire but was pursued by American aircraft to Tho Xuan. Of the crew of the F-4 shot down, flown from USS America, Radar Intercept Officer (RIO) Bernard F. Rupinski was killed but pilot Walter E. Wilber was able to eject and was captured. Wilber became an outspoken critic of American military policy while Ton would be made a Hero of the Vietnam People's Armed Forces.

MiG-17s of the 923rd Fighter Regiment were based at Tho Xuan as well. Experienced pilots Le Hai and Luu Huy Chao, having been briefed by Nguyen Van Bay, utilized the manoeuvrability of the aircraft on 14 June to each claim a F-4 destroyed. On 9 July F-8s were attacked and one was claimed destroyed by Nguyen Phi Hung who was assaulted by other F-8s and, despite much manoeuvring, was killed .

MiG-17s, accompanied by MiG-21s of the 921st Fighter Regiment flying as escorts, flew on 29 July and the former, four in number of the 923rd Fighter Regiment, became involved in a battle with F-8s. Le Hai and Luu Huy Chao were credited with a victory, however, Le Si Diep was forced to eject but did not survive. The pilots of the MiG-17s still flying were directed to break off the combat and were escorted by the MiG-21s to Tho Xuan.

During a combat on 1 August Nguyen Hong Nhi, while flying a MiG-21 beset with a malfunctioning throttle and blighted with a faulty electrical system, engaged F-8s, claiming one destroyed, but was shot down and forced to eject. On 19 September Vu Dinh Rang was dismayed to find fault with the missile firing system of the MiG-21 flown and consequently had to eject once the tail was separated from the fuselage by an AAM fired from a F-8.   Both pilots were lucky to survive entering combat with defective equipment.

On 26 October, Nguyen Dang Kinh and Vu Xuan Thieu, while flying at low level, saw aircraft and climbed to gain advantage. The USN aircraft spotted attempted to egress over the Gulf of Tonkin and both VPAF pilots fired R-3S missiles and Nguyen Dang Kinh subsequently claimed a F-4 destroyed. Ground control directed the MiG-21 pilots to beware of SAMs, but both were able to make a return to the 921st Fighter Regiment element based at Tho Xuan.

To Great Consequence

Days later, Johnson ordered an end to Rolling Thunder, effective November 1, not because objectives had been met or because of casualties suffered, but, due to domestic concerns. Political pressure was brought to bear to find a popular solution to the dilemma in the USA presented by the conflict in Vietnam so as to secure the office of the President for the Democratic Party candidate Hubert Humphrey. Negotiation with the DRV was sought and a halt was called to the bombing campaign so as to indicate a willingness to bring about a peaceful conclusion to the conflict.

Rolling Thunder had caused destruction and devastation on a scale difficult to calculate though statisticians worked to do just that. According to information compiled by the Pacific Air Forces for the Defense Technical Information Centre, the 643,000 tons of ordnance dropped in the course of the campaign resulted in the destruction of 22% of the industrial infrastructure, 47% of the transportation systems, 65% of the oils produced or stored, 58% of electrical power capacity and 73% of the military facilities of the DRV. It was left to the CIA to estimate that 90,000 casualties were inflicted, 72,000 of which were civilian.

The ADF-VPAF persevered through the Rolling Thunder assault and gained both in prowess and effect. AAA and SAMs inflicted significant losses on the USAF and USN and forced the adoption of defensive and offensive counter measures which restricted the efficacy of strikes. The VPAF was able to introduce and field the MiG-17 and the MiG-21 to great consequence; often forcing aircraft to drop ordnance and inflicting casualties on the attackers. Success came at a cost, however, in aircraft and pilots, neither of which were plentiful and the losses in machines and men were such that, at times, it was impossible to influence the events over the DRV. Yet, the VPAF, with assistance given and training applied, responded consistently to consequences suffered with persistent resistance. By the time that the Rolling Thunder campaign ended the VPAF Fighter Regiments, the 921st and the 923rd, were units operating with force and potency.

With the cessation of Rolling Thunder came hope that discussions in Paris to bring about a peace which would result in the withdrawal of American military forces from Vietnam would be successful. However, underlings of Republican presidential candidate Richard Nixon set out to sabotage the negotiations by engaging party fundraiser Anna Chenault to speak to the President of the RVN, Nguyen Van Thieu, to indicate that better terms would gained by a Republican administration than by a Democratic administration. The result of the conspiracy was that the government of the RVN withdrew from the proposed peace conference which foundered days before the American elections; Nixon defeated Humphrey and the American War continued under terms no better for anyone while casualties mounted for all.

Destroying The Drones

For the time being the DRV was not subjected to a bombing campaign.   However, aircraft were intercepted by the VPAF; reconnaissance drones sent by the American air forces to photograph sites north of the Demilitarized Zone.   The principal type encountered by Vietnamese pilots was the Ryan AQM-34 Firebee, which flew along a programmed route at a speed approaching that of sound.

Being considered targets of great importance, a drone destroyed was acknowledged as a victory to be credited and, though posing no direct threat to an attacker, such success was difficult to achieve as the aircraft, of small size and great speed, had to be detected by radar on the ground and located by the pilot in the air; very specific direction was given to be followed in order to find the drone which altered direction and altitude.

As noted, the first victory gained by a VPAF pilot flying a MiG-21 was a drone destroyed by Nguyen Hong Nhi with a R-3S missile on 4 March 1966. While pilots flying MiG-17s were able to mount successful attacks on occasion it was the MiG-21s of the 921st Fighter Regiment which were tasked with destroying the drones.

A pilot seeking a drone need not fear an enemy attack, however, perils existed nonetheless for, as Hong Bieu noted "one had to fly close to the target ... and fly the aircraft out of the gigantic zone of fire"[10] to avoid the result of a successful strike. In what may be an apocryphal tale, it was reported that one pilot intercepted a drone over the Gulf of Tonkin but, frustrated by malfunctioning R-3S missiles, had to use a wing tip as a weapon only to realize that target fixation had resulted in the loss of fuel reserve and was forced to eject. On 9 March 1971 Luong Duc Truong, flying a MiG-17 with the 923rd Fighter Regiment, destroyed a drone but afterwards crashed fatally. Apparently, in April 1971 a MiG-21 was destroyed by anti aircraft fire while in pursuit of a drone which survived such plenteous attention. Despite the hazards, one pilot, Mai Van Cuong of the 921st Fighter Regiment, became the preeminent destroyer of drones, being credited with the destruction of six. Han Vinh Tuong of the 921st Fighter Regiment was the last pilot to claim a drone downed while flying a MiG-21 following a successful interception on 6 January 1973 while Truong Cong Thanh of the 923rd Fighter Regiment was credited with the destruction of a drone when piloting a MiG-17 but did not return from the mission.

925th Fighter Regiment

In February 1969 a group of Vietnamese which had been training in the PRC to fly the Shenyang J-6, a licence built version of the MiG-19, since September 1965 arrived at Kep to establish the 925th Fighter Regiment. Le Quang Trung, who had been credited with five victories while serving with the 923rd Fighter Regiment, was transferred to and made commander of the unit. Much effort was required to set up systems to

---

[10] Hong Bieu quoted in Vùng trời kỷ niệm, Cao Bằng Online, 29/08/2012.

support the JJ-2s used to train pilots and the MiG-19s to be made operational.

As of April several pilots flying the MiG-19 were declared combat ready. Characteristics of the aircraft, the ability to climb at great speed and limited range, meant service would not be to patrol an area but to operate as a point defence in response to detected incursions. Consequently, the decision was made to move the 925th Fighter Regiment to the airbase by Yen Bai, located to the northwest of Hanoi, even though the facilities available were rudimentary.

As the American air forces were not launching strikes upon the DRV at the time, members of the unit were able to concentrate on training to improve piloting skills. Efforts were also made to maximize serviceability and develop tactics with the MiG-19 which was an aircraft significantly different from those previously operated by the VPAF. The transition by pilots who had flown the MiG-17 was made, but there were casualties. Taking off only to crash for no known reason, Duong Trung Tan was killed on 13 September. A training flight on 6 April 1970 resulted in a tragic accident when Bui Dinh Doan and Le Quang Trung collided in the air with fatal results for both. That the commander of the 925th Fighter Regiment, an ace with great experience, could die in accidental circumstances served as a sobering example of the need for great care when learning to pilot the MiG-19.

Refurbishment, Training, Memorial

The other Fighter Regiments, the 921st and the 923rd, were able to concentrate on the refurbishment of aircraft damaged in service and suffering from a harmful climate as well as the training of pilots, all with the support of advisors from the USSR, while maintaining combat readiness. Pilots practiced interceptions in conjunction with ground control and took courses to develop skills at flying in adverse weather conditions. Some who flew the MiG-17 were trained to fly the MiG-21 while others experienced on the type were trained to fly the MF version being delivered from the USSR to the 921st Fighter Regiment.

Repair and improvement was carried out at VPAF airbases, many of which had suffered great damage after being designated targets during the Rolling Thunder campaign. Defences were enhanced with additional AAA and the assignment of SAM regiments. Electrical supply systems, be they permanent installations or mobile generators, were created or distributed to support the radar systems essential to GCI. The fuel stored in the vicinity of airbases was increased and dispersed as possible. Efforts were made to deal with the shortage of trained support personnel, particularly those working with communications systems and, most important of all, those who would service aircraft.

The A-33 Aircraft Repair Facility had been established on 10 April 1961 at the Bach Mai airfield where ground crew would assemble and repair aircraft. While there was a shortage of personnel and equipment, support was provided by other socialist nations and progress was made in maintenance and serviceability as more technicians were trained. When the USAF and the USN began launching strikes upon VPAF airfields mechanics and engineers were forced to work under great strain yet, following the conclusion of the Rolling Thunder campaign, in 1968 ground crew were recognized as having refurbished 11 airframes, repaired eight aircraft as well as performed 12 engine changes and assembled 24 aircraft during the year.

On 2 September 1969, the anniversary of the independence of Vietnam, the President of the DRV and the Chairman of the Central Committee of the Worker's Party of Vietnam, Ho Chi Minh, having been ill, but apparently recovered, died abruptly. The venerable leader of both the movement to liberate Vietnam and the unification efforts of the Vietnamese was beloved by the population and accorded a memorial service on 9 September in the Ba Dinh Square of Hanoi, where Uncle Ho had made the Vietnamese Declaration of Independence, which was attended by more than 100,000 people. Overhead flew a formation of MiG-21s.

14 pilots of the 921st Fighter Regiment, had been chosen, 12 to participate in the flypast over the square, two in reserve -
1st Flight
Nguyen Hong Nhi (lead), Le Toan Thang, Pham Dinh Tuan, Nguyen Duc Soat
2nd Flight
Nguyen Van Ly (lead), Pham Phu Thai, Le Thanh Dao, Nguyen Hong My
3rd Flight
Mai Van Cuong (lead), Pham Thanh Nam, Nguyen Van Khanh, Nguyen Van Long

Reserve

Bui Duc Nhu, Dang Ngoc Ngu.

Practice flights were made in formation three times a day and one was conducted over Ba Dinh Square the day before the ceremony was to occur. On 9 September the designated pilots took off from Phuc Yen at 0900 hours. The aircraft were arranged in three ascending flights of four. Flying at an altitude of less than 300 metres (985 feet) in formation at 850 kilometres per hour (528 miles per hour), the MiG-21s appeared at Ba Dinh Square at 0930 hours and flew by the people gathered to pay homage to Ho Chi Minh accompanied by 12 MiG-17s flown by pilots of the 923rd Fighter Regiment lead by Nguyen Van Bay. Having completed the solemn task all of the pilots landed safely.

Opportunities to engage in combat were rare as, with the exception of drones, following the conclusion of the Rolling Thunder attacks, few aircraft of the American air forces were encountered in areas defended by the VPAF. On 28 January 1970, in overcast skies above the Mu Gia Pass by the border between the DRV and the KL, a Sikorsky HH-53 Super Jolly Green Giant of the 40th Aerospace Rescue and Recovery Service (ARRS) engaged in a SAR operation attempting to retrieve the crew of a F-105 shot down by anti aircraft fire was intercepted by MiG-21s of the 921st Fighter Regiment and destroyed by Vu Ngoc Dinh in the company of Pham Dinh Tuan who, while engaging F-4s flying as escort and claiming one destroyed, maneuvered into a mountain side, apparently, as a result of the inclement weather. The unit suffered a further loss on 28 March when Pham Thanh Nam was killed in an action with aircraft of Navy Fighter Squadron (VF)-142 of the USS Constellation.

Significant effort to enhance the skills and capabilities of the VPAF was made by advisors from the USSR led, from 15 October by Nikolai Sutiagin, a pilot of tremendous experience who served in the Great Patriotic War and the conflict on the Korean peninsula, there being credited with some 22 victories. Advisors concentrated on improving combat readiness while reducing malfunctions suffered and specialists offered both theoretical and practical training to pilots. An inventory of available parts and supplies was undertaken enabling objective material aid requests to be made which resulted in the establishment of a stock of equipment to improve the serviceability of aircraft within the Fighter Regiments.

A campaign was mounted by the 921st Fighter Regiment in 1971 against USAF aircraft flying over the supply lines through the KL and the Khmer Republic (KR), known to Americans as the Ho Chi Minh Trail, by which the DRV supported and supplied the NLSFV and forces fighting in the RVN. The aircraft which were attacked, the Cessna O-2 Skymaster and the North American OV-10 Bronco, operated at low speed and low altitude and proved difficult targets for pilots flying the MiG-21. Some victories were claimed but AAA proved a more effective threat to the enemy operating over the trails than an aircraft designed to intercept targets at supersonic speed at stratospheric height. Attempts were made to attack Boeing B-52 Stratofortresses conducting operations over the KL but the opportunity was infrequent and the target elusive though Vu Dinh Rang, flying a MiG-21 of the 921st Fighter Regiment was credited with damaging a B-52 on the night of 20 November. Such efforts, though of limited success, were made possible by the rejuvenation and enhancement of the VPAF undertaken in the years following the conclusion of the Rolling Thunder campaign. It became possible not only to defend Hanoi and Haiphong but to sortie eastward into the KL and fly southward toward the Demilitarized Zone.

Just such an opportunity arose on 18 December when the USAF sent a helicopter with an escort to retrieve a unit operating in the KL. A carefully coordinated GCI was carried out by a pair of MiG-21s of the 921st Fighter Regiment supported by a pair of MiG-19s of the 925th Fighter Regiment. Le Thanh Dao, of the 921st Fighter Regiment, destroyed a F-4 and left the area. The crew of the F-4, pilot Kenneth R. Johnson and WSO Samuel R. Vaughan, was able to eject and a SAR operation was mounted which proved fruitless as the two airmen became prisoners of war. Again aircraft of the two VPAF units were sent aloft on a mission of interception and in the subsequent combat a F-4 was destroyed, by Vo Sy Giap of the 921st Fighter Regiment, from which the crew of aircraft commander William T. Stanley and pilot Lester O'Brien were able to eject and later be retrieved by another SAR effort, however, following the action, a F-4 ran out of fuel forcing the ejection of the crew of pilot Kenneth R. Wells and WSO Leland L. Hildebrand both of whom were captured. A MiG-21 of the

921st Fighter Regiment was destroyed and the pilot killed, not by the enemy, but in a friendly fire incident when Nguyen Van Khanh erroneously flew into a zone designated for SAM defence.

The American air forces launched Operation Proud Deep Alpha from 26 December to 30 December, while students who could have staged protests in universities and colleges were on vacation, in an effort to destroy AAA batteries and SAM sites as well as military material stored north of the Demilitarized Zone in the DRV. The attackers endured few losses, but, the strikes were hampered by the monsoon and the effort was ineffective. As a result, however, the ADF-VPAF further enhanced the defences in place.

On 19 January 1972 Nguyen Hong My, piloting a MiG-21 of the 921st Fighter Regiment, claimed a F-4 destroyed which is believed to be the McDonnell Douglas RF-4 Phantom II flown by pilot Robert K. Mock and WSO John L. Stiles listed as a loss on 20 January by the USAF. Encounters between the ADF-VPAF and the American air forces were, again, occurring with regularity. The enhanced aerial defences of the DRV were tested and, on occasion, ironically. On 19 January, a MiG-19 was lost when ground control directed Nguyen Duc Soat to attack in error, the pilot, concerned by the appearance and behaviour of the target, asking "Are you sure these are not friendly aircraft?"[11], only to be directed to continue the attack. The R-3S missile fired ran true and Nguyen Tu Dung was fortunate to be able to eject safely. The VPAF command had not been notified by the 925th Fighter Regiment that aircraft had been sent aloft and the defences had proved all too efficient.

Blue Hill

On 3 February 1972 the 927th Blue Hill Fighter Regiment was established at Phuc Yen. Under the command of Nguyen Hong Nhi, the outfit was equipped with the MiG-21 PFM. Tho Xuan was prepared to accommodate the unit.

---

[11] Nguyen Duc Soat quoted in Toperczer, István, MiG Aces of the Vietnam War, p.165.

Dang Van Dinh, flying a MiG-21 of the 921st Fighter Regiment, engaged in a duel with an F-4, of the 555th Tactical Fighter Squadron (TFS), flown by pilot Joseph W. Kittinger II and WSO Leigh A. Hodgdon on 1 March; both fired missiles at each other but the Vietnamese pilot was forced to eject from the MiG-21 and the American crew were able to claim a victory. On 3 March a Lisunov Li-2 landing at the airbase at Vinh was hit by a SAM fired in error which killed the 22 people aboard including Le Trong Huyen who was a pilot of great experience having been officially credited with four victories while serving with the 921st Fighter Regiment. MiG-17s of the 923rd Fighter Regiment were in combat on 6 March and, while Le Hai was credited with a F-4 destroyed, Hoang Ich was killed.

Peril Great And Continual

While losses suffered were troubling, imminent events would place the pilots who flew with the four Fighter Regiments protecting the DRV in a period of peril great and continual.

Nixon had sought to establish a state of security within the RVN that would enable a withdrawal of American military units from combat roles. What was referred to as Vietnamization saw the equipping and training of the armed forces of the RVN while the war, as described by Andrew Goodpaster, was de-Americanized. Nonetheless, the NLFSV and the VPA were resilient and the ARVN, though enhanced, was unable to achieve decisive military success. Thieu was elected, by fraudulent means, to another term as President of the RVN but the grotesque violence and enforced resettlement endured by the population meant that the victory was not celebrated by the people. The revelation of the massacre of Vietnamese by American soldiers at My Lai and campaigns undertaken by American and RVN forces in the KR and the KL caused protests in the USA. Nixon resolved to negotiate a settlement with the DRV and was seeking a means to force the issue when, in the last days of the seasonal monsoon, on 30 March, the Nguyen Hue Offensive was launched by the VPA with the support of the NLFSV against the RVN. The American forces could not yet leave Vietnam in peace.

A series of deployments by the USAF under the designation Constant Guard saw the massing of units to perpetrate attacks on the

DRV. With the clearing of the weather on 5 April Operation Freedom Train was begun to strike targets north of the Demilitarized Zone and, eventually, to the 20th parallel and beyond. By 16 April bombs were, again, falling onto the Red River delta; USAF B-52s, accompanied by F-4s dropping chaff to obstruct radar and USN A-6s mounted Operation Freedom Porch Bravo to launch strikes against sites around Haiphong. Having units based within operational range, elements of the VPAF rose to defend oil storage facilities being attacked. Three MiG-21s were lost, one of which, bearing camouflage, manoeuvred vigorously before some nine missiles fired, though the three pilots, Le Khuong and Nguyen Hong My of the 921st Fighter Regiment and Duong Dinh Nghi of the 927th Fighter Regiment were able to eject safely. The USAF and USN, while causing significant damage to targets bombed, each suffered but a single loss, not to any of the MiG types sent to intercept the attackers from all of the VPAF Fighter Regiments, but to SAMs.

Hoang Quoc Dung, of the 921st Fighter Regiment, was able to destroy a F-4 of the USN flown by pilot Albert R. Molinaire and RIO James B. Souder, who became prisoners of war, on 27 April, but it had been made obvious to the ground controllers and pilots of the VPAF Fighter Regiments that the battles yet to come would be hard fought. On 6 May a pair of MiG-17s of the 923rd Fighter Regiment were in combat with USN aircraft from the USS Coral Sea and, though Nguyen Van Luc claimed a Grumman A-6 Intruder destroyed, Nguyen Van Bay, who had the same name as the ace serving as a command duty officer, was killed and later in the day MiG-21s of the 927th Fighter Regiment were at disadvantage in a battle with USN aircraft from the USS Kitty Hawk and ordered to egress by ground control but Le Van Lap was forced to eject while in the attempt. All four Fighter Regiments sortied aircraft on 8 May and Nguyen Hung Son, flying J-6 6029, and Nguyen Ngoc Tiep, flying J-6 6005 of the 925th each claimed a F-4 destroyed while Vo Si Giap of the 921st was ordered to eject after the MiG-21 flown was struck by at least one missile but did not do so in order to manoeuvre the damaged aircraft away from students gathered outside the Thuong Trung Secondary School only to die on 11 May of the injuries sustained in the resulting crash.

Made To Interfere

There had been combat aplenty with the USN, not only with aircraft, but also with ships. In 1969, elements of the VPAF command had proposed launching a strike against USN aircraft carriers but were eventually dissuaded by advisors from the USSR who believed such an effort would accomplish but little at great cost. In 1971 several pilots of the 923rd Fighter Regiment began training to make low level attacks with assistance from instructors from the RC and plans were made to interfere with the operations conducted by USN vessels against fishing boats and installations along the shore in the vicinity of Dong Hoi. The Khe Gat airbase, of diminutive dimensions, was constructed, with great secrecy along the southern coast of the DRV and on 18 April 1972 Tu De and Le Hong Diep each flew a MiG-17F from Kep, via Gia Lam and Vinh, to land there. Both aircraft had been modified by an engineer who graduated from the Zhukovsky Aviation Institute in the USSR, Truong Khanh Chau, who had designed fittings for the conveyance of 250 kilogram bombs and installed brake parachutes to enable a landing within 500 metres (1,640 feet). The 403rd Radar Company monitored the waters along the coast and reported the appearance of several USN vessels in the morning of 19 April.

Fog around Khe Gat prevented aircraft from taking off, but, later in the day, at 1605 hours, the two modified MiG-17Fs took off piloted by Le Xuan Di, flying 2019, and Nguyen Van Bay, namesake of the famous airman, flying 2047, and were directed to targets in the Gulf of Tonkin but became separated before making contact with the enemy. Nonetheless, each pilot sighted USN ships. Le Xuan Di accelerated and dove to drop two bombs when about 750 metres (2,460 feet) from the USS Higbee which was struck by both. Nguyen Van Bay passed the USS Oklahoma City and flew a reciprocal course dropping the two bombs carried in proximity. At least one SAM was fired but to no effect as Le Xuan Di landed, running into the arresting barrier at the end of the landing strip despite the brake chute, though without damage or injury to aircraft or body, to be followed by Nguyen Van Bay landing safely. The attack lasted a total of 17 minutes and would contribute to the pilots earning the title of Hero of the Vietnam People's Armed Forces; Bay, posthumously, in 1994 and Di in 2015.

Both ships were damaged, the destroyer USS Higbee significantly with a gun turret and handling room destroyed and the cruiser USS Oklahoma City slightly with antennas perforated. Eventually locating Khe Gat, USN aircraft launched a reprisal raid on 22 April in an attempt to destroy the MiG-17Fs. One was damaged necessitating disassembly and transport to a repair facility while the other was flown away as the purpose of Khe Gat had been served.

Under Tremendous Stress

Nixon ordered the commencement of the Linebacker operation on 9 May which was a campaign of bombing the DRV meant to curtail the support given to the NLFSV, prevent the supply of VPA units in the RVN and destroy targets of military value as well damage the complex system of irrigation in country. The mining of the waters in the vicinity of the harbours of Cam Pha, Hon Gay, Tanh Hoa, Vinh and Haiphong was undertaken by the USN, which, given the monicker Operation Pocket Money, was to prevent the supply of the DRV by sea. By such means Nixon hoped to bring an end to the Nguyen Hue Offensive and negotiate a withdrawal of American Forces from a RVN to be left independent and secure.

Attacks upon several VPAF airbases on 9 May foreshadowed a major effort by the American air forces the following day and the Fighter Regiments prepared accordingly. The strikes came, as anticipated, on 10 May and the first VPAF aircraft in combat were a pair of MiG-21s of the 921st Fighter Regiment, which had only just taken off at 0852 hours, having but 200 metres (656 feet) of altitude when attacked by F-4s. Nguyen Van Ngai was killed but Dang Ngoc Ngu, flying an aircraft damaged by a fuel tank jettisoned, claimed a victory. Pilots of the unit were in combat about two hours later in the vicinity of Yen Bai with F-4s and Cao Son Khao claimed one destroyed only to be killed, in error, by a SAM during the ongoing combat. A flight of MiG-19s of the 925th Fighter Regiment joined the battle. Nguyen Van Phuc made effective use of the cannon armed aircraft to shoot down the F-4 flown by a crew of vast experience, pilot Robert A. Lodge, who died, and WSO Roger C. Locher who survived to be rescued some 23 days later, but Le Duc Oanh was forced to eject and succumbed to injuries sustained. In the meantime USAF aircraft had carried out attacks on the Long Bien bridge and the Yen Vien rail yard without loss despite an intense effort mounted by the Missile Regiments. Further sorties by MiG-19s of the 925th Fighter Regiment resulted in the destruction of the F-4 flown by the crew of pilot Jeffrey L. Harris and WSO Dennis E. Wilkinson, both of whom were killed, by Le Van Tuong who, attempting to land at Yen Bai without fuel, ran off the runway to be killed in the ensuing crash. Further attacks were made, by the USN, on strategic sites about Hai Duong. A flight of four MiG-17s of the 923rd Fighter Regiment took off from Kep to engage but were set upon by F-4s of VF-96 of the USS Constellation. Do Hang was forced to eject after the MiG-17 flown, 2069, was hit by at least one missile but, while making the parachute descent, was strafed by the enemy and killed. Two other MiG-17s were destroyed; Tra Van Kiem, flying 2012, being killed and Nguyen Van Tho, flying 2036, ejecting. MiG-21s of the 927th Fighter Regiment flown by Le Thanh Dao and Vu Van Hop joined the struggle. The Vietnamese pilots, able to see trails of smoke left by American aircraft which were about to return to the aircraft carrier waiting off the coast, made an interception. Each fired a R-3S missile and both claimed a victory, Dao over the F-4 flown by the crew of pilot Harry L. Blackburn and RIO Stephen A. Rudloff who were captured, though the former subsequently died, and Hop over the F-4 flown by the crew of pilot Randall H. Cunningham and RIO Willie P. Driscoll who ejected to be rescued from the water.

The combats of 10 May were hard fought by the Americans, who claimed 11 aircraft destroyed, and the Vietnamese, who claimed six aerial victories. The reality was that the USAF and the USN each lost two F-4s while the VPAF suffered seven aircraft lost in total, three MiG-17s, two MiG-19s and two MiG-21s of which one was a victim of friendly fire. Of prime significance, however, was the use of chaff dropped to confound radar directed defence systems and of laser and electro optical guided bombs able to make strikes with great precision.

The damage caused was significant, but the Long Bien bridge had not yet been rendered impassable. A strike was mounted on 11 May by the USAF. Laser guided bombs left the structure in such a state of ruin that repair to a practical state was not possible until after the conclusion of the

American War. MiG-21s of the 927th Fighter Regiment took to the air and were able to interfere with aircraft flying on SAM suppression and CAP flights. Ngo Duy Thu despatched the F-105 flown by pilot William H. Talley and EWO James P. Padgett, both of whom became prisoners of war, then landed at Phuc Yen. Ngo Van Phu destroyed a F-4 with the crew of pilot Joseph W. Kittinger II, who, having flown some 485 sorties in theatre, had shot down a MiG-21, and WSO William J. Reich who each became prisoners of war, but, in turn, the Vietnamese pilot was made to eject by the crew of pilot Stephen E. Nichols and WSO James R. Bell flying a F-4.

Despite the concerns of command and staff over problems with communications between elements of the ADF and the VPAF as well as the necessary integration of pilots with limited experience into combat with the Fighter Regiments, tremendous aerial battles continued to occur. Flying a MiG-21, Nguyen Ngoc Hung, of the 927th, claimed a F-4 on 18 May and Do Van Lanh, of the 921st, destroyed a F-4 on 20 May, while Nguyen Duc Soat, of the 927th, benefited from capable ground control to destroy an A-7 on 23 May. Pilots of the 923rd flying the MiG-17 were also involved with Hanh Vinh Tuong claiming a F-4 on 18 May and on 23 May Vu Van Dang and Nguyen Van Dien were, together, credited with the destruction of a F-4 before being killed in an action during which Nguyen Cong Ngu was also shot down though able to eject safely. Airmen of the 925th, piloting the MiG-19, were engaged on 23 May and Vu Chinh Nghi was forced to eject, following which Nguyen Hong Son and Pham Hung Son cooperated to claim a F-4 destroyed. Not every battle of significance resulted in victories and losses though. On 26 May an attack upon storage facilities, west of Hanoi, at Son Tay, had been disrupted when first MiG-21s and then MiG-19s attacked the F-4s flying at high altitude dropping chaff. Many missiles and numerous cannon shells sought targets, though the only aircraft known to be struck was one F-4 damaged by a AAM fired by another, resulting in great confusion amongst the attackers with chaff dispersed and ordnance dropped ineffectively. Nonetheless, the American air forces had and continued to put the VPAF Fighter Regiments under tremendous stress. Nguyen Van Lung, of the 927th, was killed in a struggle with F-4s on 31 May but Pham Phu Thai, of the 921st, was given recognition for victories over F-4s on 1 June and on 10 June, but, the following day two

MiG-19s of the 925th were lost, to F-4s of the USN, and though Nguyen Hung Song was able to eject Nguyen Van Phuc was killed.

Alert And Attack

Since the commencement of Linebacker the four Fighter Regiments of the VPAF had responded to the attacks by the American air forces by massing defenders as possible. While victories had been claimed, losses incurred were significant and could not long be sustained. A conference of VPAF officers was held during the last days of May and the first days of June to analyze the situation with the resultant report distributed on 12 June and the recommendations made were applied immediately. Rather than trying to concentrate numerous aircraft from multiple Fighter Regiments in the air, pairs of aircraft were to be placed on alert and attack with the guidance of ground control. Tasks were allotted based on the qualities of the aircraft with MiG-17s, which were lacking in speed, and MiG-19s, which were lacking in endurance, flying at low altitude in the vicinity of the airbase taken off from while MiG-21s would fly at high altitude to be directed far and wide. Essentially, it was acknowledged that, while the VPAF had expanded in size and capability, the Fighter Regiments would be most effective using tactics devised during the Rolling Thunder campaign; to respond to developing situations and strike under the direction of ground control when at advantage rather than defend and accept combat when attacked. Deciding just which aircraft to intercept with the limited resources of the VPAF proved crucial to success. USN strikes, which incorporated escorts flown by crews trained at the Top Gun Fighter Weapons School, coordinated to be brief in duration, were difficult to intercept so it was determined that the Fighter Regiments were most effective when USAF strikes made up of bombers carrying laser and electro optical guided bombs surrounded by masses of other aircraft flying in various support roles were engaged. As well, it was recognized that the immediate environs of Haiphong and Hanoi were better defended by AAA and SAMs while the Fighter Regiments were best utilized in attack against USAF aircraft arriving laden with ordnance or leaving short of fuel.

Success followed the distribution of the report; Pham Phu Thai and Do Van Lanh, of the 921st Fighter Regiment were credited with victories over F-4s on 13 June. Further victories were recorded for the unit by Do Van Lanh on the 21st and the 24th and by Pham Phu Thai on the 24th and the 27th of the month. 27 June proved to be a day of particular adversity for the USAF. Bui Duc Nhu, flying a MiG-21 of the 927th Fighter Regiment, claimed a F-4 destroyed to the west of Hanoi early in the morning. The crew of pilot John P. Cerak and WSO David B. Dingee, both of whom had flown hundreds of sorties in theatre, were able to eject prompting the mounting of a SAR mission though the two airmen would be captured. In the meantime a chaff dropping F-4 was destroyed flown by pilot Farrell J. Sullivan, who was killed, and WSO Richard L. Francis, who became a prisoner of war, by an element of the 927th Fighter Regiment made up of Ngo Duy Thu and Nguyen Duc Soat, each of which were credited with a victory. MiG-21s of the 921st Fighter Regiment were directed to interfere with the SAR effort in the vicinity of the border between the DRV and the KL. Bui Thanh Liem then Pham Phu Thai each fired an R-3S missile, each of which destroyed a F-4 and though both pilots, Lynn A. Aikman and R.C. Miller, were subsequently rescued the two WSOs, Thomas J. Hanton and Richard H. McDow, became prisoners of war as did the two airmen whose ejections instigated the rescue operation. Four F-4s had been destroyed by the MiG-21 equipped Fighter Regiments with no loss of men or machines.

Further success for came on 5 July when Ha Vinh Thanh and Nguyen Tien Sam of the 927th Fighter Regiment attacked escorts of a strike utilizing laser guided bombs east of Kep. Such weapons required the attacking aircraft to remain in the area to direct the fall of the bombs. Climbing through overcast Thanh and Sam, one behind the other, were each able to fire a pair of missiles at F-4s. Both targets were hit and the crews ejected to become prisoners. Thanh dove into the cloud cover but Sam had to fly through the explosion of the target and the MiG-21 flown consequently lost power. Fortunately Sam was able to restart the engine and make a safe landing as Thanh had done.

USAF aircraft were able to claim success on 8 July when a vehicle repair facility in Hanoi was attacked. Dang Ngoc Nhu and Tran Viet, of the 921st Fighter Regiment, were engaged by F-4s escorting the strike and, though the latter was able to cause the destruction of one of the enemy and land essentially without fuel, the former was killed. The 927th Fighter Regiment suffered loss as well when both Nguyen Ngoc Hung and Vu Duc Hop, suffering from inadequate ground control, were set upon by the proficient F-4 crew of pilot Richard S. Ritchie and WSO Charles B. DeBellevue to be shot down and killed.

Three pilots killed in a day was a blow to the VPAF and all the more so as Dang Ngoc Nhu, having been trained in the USSR from 1961, had amassed great experience being first being credited with a victory on 13 August 1966 and ultimately with a success on 10 May 1972, the seventh. Concerned that the pilots of the VPAF approached combat with the American air forces without fear, the Central Committee of the Workers Party of Vietnam directed that courage be tempered with a pragmatic approach incorporating analysis of battles fought and the development of tactics to be used as a means of limiting casualties. Nonetheless, casualties continued to mount; on 18 July Nguyen The Duc of the 927th Fighter Regiment was killed when attacked by an F-4 while attempting to land at Gia Lam.

Over the last days of July members of the 927th Fighter Regiment engaged the enemy several times. On 24 July Nguyen Tien Sam downed a F-4 over Kep then landed at Phuc Yen to run out of fuel on the runway while Le Thanh Dao and Truong Ton each claimed a F-4 destroyed east of Hanoi but, with but little fuel remaining, were directed to fly on low consumption but high anxiety mode to Phuc Yen and Kep respectively. Nguyen Tien Sam was able to shoot down a F-4 but Nguyen Thanh Xuan was forced to eject on 29 July while on 30 July Nguyen Duc Soat so damaged a F-4 of the USAF that the crew of pilot G. B. Brooks and WSO James M. McAdams abandoned the aircraft over the Gulf of Tonkin to be rescued by the USN.

Despite poor weather limiting the number of strikes mounted by the American air forces, August proved a difficult month for the VPAF. The 921st Fighter Regiment suffered losses on the 10th as Nguyen Ngoc Thien was killed and on the 12th when Nguyen Cong Huy was forced to eject. The 927th Fighter Regiment endured casualties on the 15th when Nguyen Hung Thong was made to eject and on the 19th as Nguyen Thang Duoc ejected only to be hunted down by the crews of two F-4s which damaged the opened parachute resulting in what would be a fatal injury. Nguyen Duc Soat and Nguyen Van Toan were each able to claim the destruction of a F-4 when elements of the 927th Fighter Regiment were in the thick of combat on 26 August though Le Van Kien had to abandon the MiG-21 flown due to a lack of fuel following an inconclusive battle with another F-4. USAF aircrew had benefitted from a device known as Combat Tree which enabled the identification of an aircraft located on radar by registering the presence of a specific identification apparatus, a friend or foe transponder, as Vietnamese and the creation of a control centre at Nakhon Phanom in the KT, known as Teaball which collected and disseminated relevant data from all available sources and issued warnings in respect of VPAF activity which was a service that USN aircrew had had available for years provided by a ship in the Gulf of Tonkin under the designation Red Crown.   There were limitations to the use of both systems, but the technical and systemic improvements did create a counter of sorts for USAF flyers to the ground control of such benefit to the Vietnamese pilots.

In September the USAF began to make the effort to mount two strikes a day. Though the VPAF was lacking in resources there was no choice but to counter as possible. The 925th Fighter Regiment was in action with the MiG-19 on 2 September; Phung Van Quang, flying the type modified to mount A-72 missile launchers armed with the 9K32 Strela-2 in addition to the cannon armament, claimed a F-105 destroyed, not by missile but by cannon, while Hoang Cao Bong had to eject. Another MiG-19 and several MiG-21s were lost through the month but all of the pilots were able to safely eject. On 9 September both of the MiG-21 equipped Fighter Regiments claimed a F-4 destroyed. Further victories were recorded, by pilots of the 927th Fighter Regiment; F-4s destroyed by Le Thanh Dao and Tran Van Nam on the 11th and by Nguyen Tien Sam on the 12th.

During the combat of 16 September between aircraft of the 555th TFS and a MiG-21 of the 927th Fighter Regiment the crews of two F-4s experienced an all too common situation with American missile systems when firing, or attempted to fire, some 12 missiles, those being, four AIM-7s and eight AIM-9Js. Only the last missile that was launched, a AIM-9J, registered a hit which destroyed the target from which Ngo Duy

Thu was able to eject. During a battle on 30 September between F-4s and MiG-21s of the 921st Fighter Regiment some 18 missiles were fired without result by both of the opposing forces. Only one aircraft was claimed destroyed, a F-4, by Tran Viet of the 921st Fighter Regiment. The R-3S, with a range of 2 kilometres (1.2 miles) at low altitude and 9 kilometres (5.6 miles) at high altitude had proved an effective weapon as utilized by the VPAF. Nonetheless, Vietnamese pilots did suffer reliability issues with the missile which was, after all, reverse engineered from the AIM-9B manufactured for the American air forces.

Ever Resilient

The attritional nature of the aerial combat over the Red River placed great strain on the VPAF, the effectiveness of which was limited by the numbers of pilots and aircraft available, but the American air forces were frustrated by the regular interception of and destruction of strike aircraft which necessitated the development and application of complex systems and planning. On 1 October a series of attacks were mounted against VPAF airbases in an effort to neutralize the Fighter Regiments, however, Le Thanh Dao of the 927th was able to claim a F-4 shot down during a battle when both the opposing forces again suffered from the erratic behaviour of missiles. Several pilots of the 927th Fighter Regiment sortied on 5 October and Bui Duc Nhu was able to claim the destruction of a F-4 in the vicinity of Yen Bai while Nguyen Tien Sam was warned by ground control of the presence of enemy aircraft to the rear and, taking advantage of the maneuverability of the MiG-21, turned inside the formation of four F-4s and fired two R-3S missiles, one of which struck the aircraft of pilot Keith H. Lewis and WSO John H. Alpers who both ejected to become prisoners of war. There was further combat the following day and interceptions by MiG-19s of the 925th Fighter Regiment based at Gia Lam and MiG-21s of the 927th Fighter Regiment based at Phuc Yen caused five of six flights of F-4s sent to bomb to drop ordnance ineffectively. Two of the MiG-21 pilots were each able to cause the destruction of a F-4; Nguyen Van Nghia so damaging the target that the crew of pilot J.P. White and WSO A.G. Egge were forced to eject over the border between the KL and the KT to be rescued and Tran Van Nam firing a first missile to no effect and a second missile which destroyed the aircraft of pilot Robert D. Anderson, who was presumed killed, and WSO George F. Latella, who became a prisoner of war. One casualty was suffered, however, as Nguyen Hung Viet of the 925th Fighter Regiment was killed diving in the pursuit of a F-4 when the MiG-19 piloted was flown directly into the ground.

Despite the loss, by mounting a spirited defence only days after the significant bombing of airbases, the VPAF was proven ever resilient. On 8 October Duong Dinh Nghi and Nguyen Van Nghia, of the 927th Fighter Regiment, attacked F-4s and though the former was forced to eject several bombers were made to drop ordnance while the latter was able to land at Phuc Yen having

> dived to an altitude of just 15 - 20 metres ... pursued all the way by four F-4s. They fired missiles and 20 millimetre shells at me but all missed. At such an altitude the enemy dared not fly lower than me so they had to shoot from above. This meant that heat-seeking missiles would be misled by the heat from the ground, while radar guided missiles would have their guidance systems jammed by the ground clutter. And firing their cannon at me was just a wast of ammunition since my flying speed was about 1300 kilometres per hour, ruling the gun out as an option[12].

Elsewhere, in Paris, where a peace conference had been in progress, diplomat Le Duc Tho announced that the DRV was prepared to accept many of the conditions proposed by negotiators of the USA. For the time being the American air forces continued to launch strikes and the VPAF continued to defend. Pilots of the 927th Fighter Regiment were often in combat mid month; on the 12th Nguyen Duc Soat destroyed a F-4 but Nguyen Tien Sam ejected and on the 13th Mai Van Tue was killed while on the 15th Le Thanh Dao ejected only to be attacked while descending by parachute. "A Phantom fired a burst ... to make many holes in my parachute", resulting in a fall at great speed with the result that "I was

---

[12] Nguyen Van Nghia quoted in Toperczer, István, MiG-21 Aces Of The Vietnam War, p. 99.

unconscious for two days and both legs [and] vertebra were broken"[13] and facing a lengthy recovery. Pham Phu Thai of the 921st Fighter Regiment, apparently attempting to protect a helpless comrade by circling the parachute, was attacked and forced to eject. The defenders had not fought in vain, though, as several F-4s had been made to drop bomb loads short of target. On 23 October raids on the DRV north of the 20th parallel were stopped ending Linebacker, an operation during which 155,548 tons of bombs had been dropped.

Yet Another Defence

In Paris an agreement had been drafted whereby the governments of the DRV and the RVN, as well as the National Liberation Front would form a tripartite commission, known as the National Council of Reconciliation and Concord, that would oversee elections to be held. Such a compromise enabled the negotiation of a withdrawal of military forces of the USA from Vietnam while the forces of the VPA and ARVN held the positions occupied. However, before what was drafted could become reality, the government of the RVN, at the insistence of Thieu who balked at the prospect of the opposing armed forces remaining in place, withdrew from the proceedings with the support of Nixon and the agreed to treaty was not signed; despite a claim made by advisor to Nixon, Henry Kissinger, peace was not yet at hand. The Americans demanded that the agreement reached be opened to allow further negotiation while support to the military forces of the RVN was increased and B-52s struck targets in the DRV. Negotiators, the government and the people of the DRV were intransigent and incensed as yet another defence had to be mounted. Linebacker II was instigated to cause maximum possible destruction in the areas of Hanoi and Haiphong and thereby result in concessions to satisfy the governments of both the RVN and the USA while proving the conviction of the latter to the former. Bombing sorties would be flown at night by B-52s with the support of numerous aircraft including Boeing

---

[13] Le Thanh Dao quoted in Toperczer, István, Silver Swallows And Blue Bandits, p. 152.

KC-135 Stratotankers, General Dynamics F-111 Aardvarks, F-105s and F-4s as escort.

Some 129 B-52s were able to attack the DRV on 18 December and at 1925 hours F-111s struck Phuc Yen and the 921st Fighter Regiment responded in spite of the attack. Tran Cung took of at 1928 hours to attempt an intercept but the signal jamming emitted by the B-52s prevented contact and a subsequent sortie undertaken by Pham Tuan from 1947 hours brought no success either but the MiG-21 flown was damaged upon landing as bombs dropped by B-52s had struck the runway used. Three B-52s, destroyed by SAMs, and a F-111 were lost by the USAF through the night. While each element of the ADF-VPAF strived as possible to down the foe, it was the Missile Regiments which proved most capable of battling the B-52s. Few pilots of the VPAF had the training necessary to engage in interceptions at night and the MiG-21s in service had limited radar capability, nonetheless, every effort was made. Two pilots were credited with downing B-52s. Pham Tuan, of the 921st Fighter Regiment, flying MiG-21MF 5121 on 27 December closed to sight a bomber then fired missiles before diving away while looking up to see the target burning. Vu Xuan Thieu, of the 927th Fighter Regiment, flying MiG-21MF 5146 on 28 December, fired missiles at a target and closed to fire cannon shells but died in the aircraft apparently damaged by debris from the explosion of the target. Each pilot was made a Hero Of The Vietnam People's Armed Forces; the body of Thieu was never found but Tuan would go on to become a cosmonaut and fly on Soyuz 37 and thus earn the title of Hero Of The Soviet Union.

VPAF units remained active in the daylight hours as the American air forces continued to intrude over the DRV though impeded by poor weather. Pilots of the 927th Fighter Regiment were in action on 23 December and Nguyen Van Nghia claimed a F-4 destroyed. Tran Viet, of the 921st Fighter Regiment, was directed towards a formation of F-4s on 27 December and, apparently, was able to down that flown by pilot Carl H. Jeffcoat and WSO Jack R. Trimble who ejected to become prisoners of war.

On 28 December, accompanying Le Van Ken, Hoang Tam Hung intercepted a reconnaissance being conducted by a North American RA-5 Vigilante and destroyed the aircraft with a R-3S missile. The two pilots of the 927th Fighter Regiment were then attacked by flights of F-4s and became separated. They were ordered to disengage and land at Phuc Yen, which Ken was able to do but Hung pursued and claimed a F-4 destroyed yelling out "He's burning!"[14] only to be killed when the MiG-21PFM 5013 flown was struck by a missile.

Airbases of the VPAF were targets of the USAF during Linebacker II. Bombs fell upon Gia Lam, Kep, Yen Lai, and again, upon Phuc Yen on 28 December. However, an airbase had been constructed at Cam Thuy to the south of Hanoi to where aircraft had previously been flown thereby escaping damage or destruction.

A final assault by B-52s was made on 29 December with concentrated attacks upon SAM storage sites and the Lang Dang rail yard. While attempting to find a cell of B-52s, at 2349 hours, Bui Doan Do of the 921st Fighter Regiment detected a F-4 and after firing two R-3S missiles claimed the target destroyed. Linebacker II was ended at 0659 hours 30 December.

Both the government of the DRV and the government of the USA claimed success in the Linebacker II campaign. The ADF-VPAF were able to shoot down several B-52s during the Dien Bien Phu in the skies while the USAF, with assistance from the United States Marine Corps (USMC) and the USN, managed to deliver a vast amount of ordnance to many targets, B-52s alone dropping some 15,000 tons of bombs, which injured 3,327 and killed 4,025 people the majority of which being civilians.

By 2 January 1973 discussions were being undertaken in Paris and progress was made culminating in an agreement on 27 January. What had been agreed to before was, essentially, agreed to again as, with the opposing military forces left in the areas occupied, the RVN and the DRV determined to unify, with the National Liberation Front, Vietnam by peaceful means. Once the Agreement on Ending the War and Restoring Peace in Vietnam, was signed, the USA pledged not to interfere in the affairs of the Vietnamese people and to contribute towards reconstruction.

There had been aerial combat while the negotiations progressed. The USAF downed a MiG-21 of the 921st Fighter Regiment, from which Bui Doan Do ejected, on 8 January and the USN destroyed a MiG-17 of the

---

[14] Hoang Tam Hung quoted in Toperczer, István, Silver Swallows And Blue Bandits, p. 165.

923rd Fighter Regiment, in which Luu Kim Ngo was killed, on 12 January. Hoang Mai Vuong and To Nhat Bai, both flying MiG-17s with the 923rd Fighter Regiment, were credited with the destruction of an AQM-34 on 8 January and 19 January respectively.

Then, over the Red River, after years of struggle, the gold star, borne on the aircraft of the Fighter Regiments of the Vietnamese People's Air Force, rose triumphant and flew unopposed.

Just What Was Achieved

Upon creation, the Fighter Regiments of the VPAF had four principal problems to surmount. Suitable aircraft to defend the DRV had to be obtained and personnel had to be trained to fly and to maintain the aircraft utilized.   Once committed to combat with the enemy it was necessary both to develop effective tactics to use and to respond to the technological developments made by the attacking air forces.

The VPAF had no viable alternative to the acceptance of aircraft designed and built in the USSR and the licence built versions of such made available by the PRC. The MiG-15UTI and the MiG-17 types, which, though obsolescent, were the original equipment of the 921st Fighter Regiment proved effective at the tasks assigned and were handy and hardy. Versions of the MiG-21 and the MiG-19 gave the VPAF expanded capabilities and, while the later proved difficult to learn to fly and hard to maintain, the former was durable and was the most effective type employed. However, maintaining a supply of aircraft able to sortie when needed proved difficult. The operations of the Fighter Regiments were always limited by an inadequate amount of serviceable aircraft available. The husbanding of resources was necessary and, thus, following excessive use or significant losses it was necessary to limit operations until aircraft on strength could be returned to a capable condition or additional aircraft were obtained.

That much training of pilots could be done in the USSR and the PRC, free of interference from the American air forces, was a boon and graduates of the schools in those countries returned to service in the DRV regularly. Though the rate of fatality was significant among the Fighter Regiments, pilots that were able to eject safely were generally able to return to duty and, as Luu Huy Chao noted, "part of my confidence came from knowing that if I had to bail out I would be landing in my own country"[15]. Once having accepted battle in 1965 until the end of the American War in 1973, while limited by the number of aircraft available for operations, the Fighter Regiments of the VPAF were never without pilots.

As attackers, the American air forces had the initiative and, as defenders, the command of the VPAF could only respond as was possible. The pilots, defending their homeland, were generally convinced of victory and flew with aggression despite facing tremendous odds and thereby often suffered losses otherwise unnecessary and, as a result, orders were issued to curtail reckless attacks. Tactics had to be and were modified regularly so as to best respond to raids launched by a vast number aircraft of varying capabilities while minimizing losses so, with the assistance of advisors from the USSR, ground control worked closely with pilots to develop effective tactics which found advantage from the particular capabilities of the types used to intercept the enemy.

Adequately countering the technical developments introduced by the American air forces, which enhanced the effectiveness of strikes, was beyond the capability of the industry of the DRV. As well as determination and persistence, the Fighter Regiments of the VPAF relied on ever increasing operational experience. Advisors and equipment from the USSR did enable the establishment of a practical defensive network based on detection and the coordination of the distinct elements of the ADF-VPAF, but the pilots of the Fighter Regiments fought without technological advantage.

Considering the limitations and difficulties which confronted the defenders of the sky over the Red River, just what was achieved was remarkable. In addition to problems of supply and the complexities of training, as well as the concerns about tactics and technology, was the matter of just how many aircraft of the foe were attacking. On any given day the USAF or the USN could make airborne over the DRV more aircraft than possessed by all of the Fighter Regiments of the VPAF combined which made the precise direction of ground control, to maximize potential and minimize risk, essential to assure both success and survival.

---

[15] Luu Huy Chao quoted in Appy, Christian G., ed., Patriots The Vietnam War Remembered From All Sides, p. 214.

The goal of an interception was to cause a strike aircraft either to drop ordnance or to be destroyed. Numerous were the bombs that could not be dropped on targets and many were the aircraft shot down. Periods of sustained success by the pilots of the VPAF meant that the American air forces had to allot aircraft as escorts which could have participated in the strike on a target.

Such was the scale of the assault that the American air forces could not be driven from the skies above the Red River, yet, neither were the Fighter Regiments of the VPAF defeated; the continued resistance of the Fighter Regiments, regularly demonstrated before both the people of the DRV and the crews of the attacking aircraft, was a remarkable triumph in and of itself.

Aftermath

Remaining American military forces withdrew from the RVN and prisoners of war left the DRV while a military detachment remained in Saigon to protect the American Embassy. The ceasefire was violated when, rather than cooperate in the effort to reach a political settlement, ARVN forces attacked elements of the NLFSV. Eventually continual aggression prompted a military response from the VPA which proved unstoppable and the opportunity to ultimately conclude the conflict was taken decisively. Despite possessing well equipped military forces the government of the RVN, lacking popular support, was unable to mount an effective defence. Thieu resigned following which the forces of the VPA entered Saigon on 30 April 1975 to end the fighting and the date of the absolute liberation has been annually celebrated as Reunification Day in Vietnam.

The Fighter Regiments of the VPAF remained based in the DRV though an element of the 923rd Fighter Regiment, known as the Invincible Flight, was detached to fly Cessna A-37 Dragonflies that had been captured to attack the Tan Son Nhat airbase on 28 April and the 935th Dong Nai Fighter Regiment was formed on 30 May to operate the Northrop F-5 Freedom Fighter many of which had been taken possession of. Rather, in the aftermath of the conflict the repair of airbases and the refurbishment of equipment, though a daunting task, was undertaken.

Unfortunately, erstwhile allies attacked resulting in further conflict. Aggressive actions by forces of Democratic Kampuchea (DK) against the DRV causing the death of Vietnamese citizens resulted in a deployment of MiG-21s to an airbase at Pakse in the Lao People's Democratic Republic from where a strike was carried out on Siem Reap on 25 February 1976 and additional assaults resulted in a reprisal by MiG-21MFs.   Continued incursions ultimately prompted an invasion of the DK which was supported by MiG-21s and Shenyang J-6s as well as by, apparently, A-37s and F-5s of the VPAF.

On 2 July 1976 the unified country was declared the Socialist Republic of Vietnam.

Political tensions resulted in occasional attacks by forces of the PRC of greater and lesser intensity over a period of years. Aerial combat did not feature in the disputes which were eventually resolved and peace was finally established in the region. The Fighter Regiments of the VPAF continue to serve as an unchallenged force protecting Vietnam.

Aircraft Inventory Of The Fighter Regiments

The Limited Number Of Aircraft

Interceptions of attacking aircraft by the Fighter Regiments of the VPAF were hampered, throughout the American War, by the limited number of aircraft available for operations due to supply, serviceability and losses. Losses that were incurred in a single day, such as 2 January 1967 when five MiG-21s were lost or 10 May 1972 when a total of seven aircraft were destroyed, affected the subsequent number of sorties that could be mounted. The frequent flights by aircraft and the limited number of ground crew with technical expertise meant that not all aircraft on strength were available for operations. Once attacks commenced on the airbases of the VPAF, aircraft could be, and were, damaged or destroyed on the ground. It was deemed wise to disperse aircraft amongst purpose built bunkers and airbases used by the VPAF, which complicated servicing and repair, and the airbase at Xiangyun in the PRC was used as a haven to store an inventory of aircraft. By 1972 the four existing Fighter Regiments may have had a combined strength in excess of 50 aircraft but the number capable of sortieing on any given day was less.

The Mikoyan-Gurevich MiG-15UTI

At least four MIG-15UTIs were delivered from the USSR by 1966 as were some from the PRC in and after 1969 which may have been MiG-15UTIs and, or, Shenyang JJ-2s, a licence built version. The aircraft were employed by the 910th Training Regiment, the 921st Fighter Regiment and the 923rd Fighter Regiment as well as by the 925th Fighter Regiment. Serviceability issues with Shenyang J-6s meant that pilots of the 925th Fighter Regiment flew Shenyang JJ-2s to improve flying proficiency.

The Mikoyan-Gurevich MiG-17

Some 32 MiG-17s were provided to the VPAF by the USSR as were an amount of the Shenyang J-5, a licence built version of the MiG-17F, by the PRC which also supplied at least one Shenyang FT-5, a two seat trainer based up the MiG-15 UTI and the MiG-17, to be used by the 910th Training Regiment. In addition several, perhaps as many as 28, of an all weather type, either the MiG-17PF or the Shenyang F-5A licence built version of the MiG-17PF, were received by the VPAF sometime between 1965 and 1966. As many as 100 of various versions of the MiG-17 may have served with the VPAF in either the 921st Fighter Regiment and, or, the 923rd Fighter Regiment through the American War.

The Mikoyan-Gurevich MiG-19

While some MiG-19Ss may have been provided for the VPAF by the USSR, at least 44 and as many as 60 Shenyang J-6s, the licence built version of the MiG-19S made in the PRC, were made available from February 1969 to equip the 925th Fighter Regiment.

The Mikoyan-Gurevich MiG-21

12 MiG-21s were delivered to the VPAF in August 1965 followed by 22 MiG-21s which were sent sometime in 1966; all were of the PFL type and were built in Plant No.30 in Moscow. 20 MiG-21F-13s, that had been built in Plant No.21 in Gorky, were taken on from June 1967; 24 of the type were sent by the RC in 1967. From October 1967, some 100 MiG-21PFMs were supplied with the last of the deliveries being made in 1972. A total of 60 MiG-21MFs, which were built in both Plant No.30 in Moscow and Plant 21 in Gorky, were ultimately delivered with the first accepted in December 1971 and the last arriving after the reunification of Vietnam in 1975. Deliveries of versions of the MiG-21U, including the US and the UM, which sat a pilot and an instructor for training purposes, manufactured in Plant 31 in Tbilisi, began in 1965 and totalled more than 20 in number. As many as 250 MiG-21s, of a variety of versions were in service with the 921st Fighter Regiment and the 927th Fighter Regiment during the American War

Photographs Of
Aircraft And Pilots

Dao Dinh Luyen entering a a MiG-17, possibly Shenyang J-5 2011, bedecked with at least nine red stars. Having commanded a group of pilot trainees in the PRC, he became the first commander of the 921st Air Regiment, leading aircraft of the unit from Mengzi in the PRC to Phuc Yen in the DRV, on Operation Project X-1, on 6 August 1964. Luyen, born in 1929, in 1977 became the commander in chief of the VPAF, died in 1999 and was made a Hero of the Vietnam People's Armed Forces on 1 December 2014.

Le Hong Diep of the 923rd Fighter Regiment boards MiG-17F 2043 at Gia Lam, on 3 January 1968 to intercept a strike on railways in the vicinity of Hanoi. During the ensuing combat with the 433 TFS of the 8 TFW Diep was forced to eject. It would seem that the MiG-17 had been hit by cannon fire from the F-4D flown by aircraft commander Bernard J. Bogoslofski and pilot Richard L. Huskey.

Mai Duc Toai aboard MiG-17F 2044, possibly serial 1088. Toai, who served with the 923rd Fighter Regiment, would ultimately be credited with two official victories, apparently an A-4 on 16 August 1966, when flying with Nguyen Van Bien and a F-105 on 25 April 1967, in cooperation with the other members of the flight flown with, Hoang Van Ky, Le Hai and Luu Huy Chao. Mai Duc Toai was made the commander of the 925th Fighter Regiment in 1970.

MiG-17s of the 923rd Fighter Regiment about to be started at Kep in 1966. In the foreground, 2055 was a camouflaged Shenyang J-5 which would be flown by Le Hai when a victory over a F-4 was claimed on 19 November 1967. Behind are four other MiG-17 types, 2001 is believed to have been a grey F type, possibly serial 1088.

MiG-17s, elegant in line, of the 923rd Fighter Regiment at Kep, including MiG-17F 2077 in the centre of the row of five, have been moved out of revetments and readied for pilots who are walking to the mounts in April 1967, a month when several of the unit would claim victories.

At Kep in June 1967 pilots of the 923rd Fighter Regiment approach camouflaged MiG-17s which have been prepared by ground crew to take to the air.

Assisted by the ground crew, the pilots have boarded the aircraft. Vu The Xuan sits in MiG-17F 2077. The same aircraft had been flown, without camouflage, by Phan Van Tuc on 21 June 1966, when two victories were claimed over the USN and may have been flown by Vo Van Mann, with camouflage, on 19 July 1967 when a victory was claimed over the USAF. Vu The Xuan would claim a victory on 19 December 1967. Four other MiG-17 types form the line including 2073, thought to be a F type and 3020, a Shenyang F-5, which was flown by Le Hai to claim victories on 14 June 1968 and 3 August 1969.

Four of a version of the MiG-17, including 3003 and 3001 with the former believed to be a Shenyang F-5 as it seems to bear insignia of the People's Liberation Army Air Force which has been overpainted with VPAF insignia.

Members of the 925th Fighter Regiment pose for photographs at Yen Bai. The pilots wear DRV armbands which, were any of them forced to eject, would indicate their nationality to any people that might suspect otherwise. An officer demonstrates tactical manoeuvres with models before 6023, 6032, 6025, 6027 and 6024, all of which are thought to be versions of the MiG-19 built in the PRC, thus Shenyang F-6s.

MiG-21PFL 4128, serial 771914, of the 921st Fighter Regiment, resplendent in the sunlight, bearing numbers as well as national markings, on both the fuselage and upper surface of the wings which are, as of yet, essentially free from the effects of weathering. It is believed that the aircraft, armed with two R-3S missiles, is being prepared for take off from Phuc Yen with Dong Van De at the controls on 4 December 1966. Though no victories were claimed that day, he would be credited with two F-105s shot down on 14 December. De, who was the son of Major General Dong Bay Cong, was the first pilot trained to fly the MiG-21 in the DRV, attained the rank of Senior Lieutenant, but lost his life in combat when flying a MiG-21 which was shot down with an AIM-7 missile fired from the F-4C flown by aircraft commander Richard M. Pascoe and pilot Norman E. Wells on 6 January 1967.

Among the most famous aircraft of the VPAF, MiG-21PFL 4326, serial 772111, of the 921st Fighter Regiment photographed at Phuc Yen is preserved at the Air Defence - Air Force Museum in Hanoi. The 13 victories marked on the aircraft were scored by a variety of pilots including Nguyen Dang Kinh, Nguyen Hong Nhi and Nguyen Van Coc. Behind is MiG-21PFM 5034 which was lost in combat on 29 July 1972 when flown by Nguyen Thanh Xuan who was able to eject. Armed, dangerous and on the move is MiG-21PFM 5015 which was adorned with a distinctive camouflage scheme on the upper surfaces and known to have been flown by Dang Ngoc Ngu, Dinh Ton, Nguyen Dang Kinh, Nguyen Tien Sam, Nguyen Van Coc and Pham Thanh Ngan. Specific aircraft, such 4326 and 5015, were maintained to the highest level by ground crew and entrusted to pilots of the greatest skill.

In the foreground of a row of MiG-21s of the 921st Fighter Regiment, before a U version of the aircraft, F-13 4429 and F-13 4422 are being prepared to sortie from Phuc Yen. Both are believed to be of a batch delivered to the DRV from the RC via the USSR which were serviced by ground crew and flown by pilots from the DPRK of Group Z. Proletarian internationalism indeed!

Pilots rush to MiG-21s in line at Phuc Yen. PFM 5006 is to the fore while eleven other MiG-21s, including one painted in a camouflaged scheme, complete the line. Visible are PFM 5025 which was flown by Bui Duc Nhu, of the 927th Fighter Regiment to claim a F-4 destroyed on 5 October 1972, being the last of three victories officially credited to the pilot, and PFM 5013 which was destroyed by an AAM fired from the F-4 flown by the crew of pilot Scott Davis and RIO Jeff Ulrich on 28 December 1972, resulting in the death of Hoang Tam Hung of the 927th Fighter Regiment who had just claimed the destruction of a RA-5 and a F-4 which were the first and the last victories credited.

Pilots and ground crew stand ready for inspection before MiG-21PFMs, armed and, apparently, ready to take to the air, with 5006 closest to the photographer and 5032 and 5030 beyond. MiG-21PFM 5006 had to be abandoned by Le Van Kien after running out of fuel following combat on 26 August 1972 while MiG-21PFM 5030 was piloted by Pham Thanh Ngan to down the F-102 flown by Wallace L. Wiggins, who was killed, on 3 February 1968.

Pilots run to MiG-21s at Phuc Yen in 1972. At least three variants of the MiG-21 are visible; 5127, the first in line, is a MF, 5903, the second in line is a UM, 5122, the third in line, is a MF and 5077, the sixth in line, is a US which was delivered to the VPAF in 1968. It appears that three of the aircraft are camouflaged.

Dang Ngoc Nhu, of the 921st Fighter Regiment, officially credited with 7 victories.

Do Van Lanh, of the 921st and 923rd Fighter Regiments, officially credited with 4 victories.

Lam Van Lich, sitting in a MiG-17, of the 921st and 923rd Fighter Regiments, officially credited with 3 victories.

Le Hai, of the 923rd Fighter Regiment, officially credited with 6 victories.

Le Thanh Dao, of the 921st and 927th Fighter Regiments, officially credited with 6 victories.

Luu Huy Chao, of the 923rd Fighter Regiment, officially credited with 6 victories.

Mai Van Cuong, of the 921st Fighter Regiment, officially credited with 8 victories.

Nguyen Dang Kinh, of the 921st and 927th Fighter Regiments, officially credited with 6 victories.

Nguyen Duc Soat, of the 921st and 927th Fighter Regiments, officially credited with 6 victories.

Nguyen Hong Nhi, of the 921st and 927th Fighter Regiments, officially credited with 8 victories.

Nguyen Hong Son, behind a MiG-19, of the 925th Fighter Regiment, officially credited with 1 victory.

Nguyen Hung Son, inspecting the fuselage mounted cannon of Shenyang J-6 6029, of the 925th Fighter Regiment, officially credited with 1 victory.

Nguyen Ngoc Do, of the 921st Fighter Regiment, officially credited with 6 victories.

Nguyen Nhat Chieu, of the 921st and 927th Fighter Regiments, officially credited with 6 victories.

Nguyen Tien Sam, of the 921st and 927th Fighter Regiments, officially credited with 5 victories.

Nguyen Van Bay, of the 921st and 923rd Fighter Regiments, officially credited with 7 victories.

Nguyen Van Coc, of the 921st Fighter Regiment, officially credited with 9 victories.

Nguyen Van Nghia, of the 927th Fighter Regiment, officially credited with 5 victories.

Pham Hung Son, in a MiG-19, of the 925th Fighter Regiment, officially credited with 1 victory.

Pham Thanh Ngan, of the 921st Fighter Regiment, officially credited with 8 victories.

Vu Ngoc Dinh, of the 921st Fighter Regiment, officially credited with 6 victories.

Nguyen Nhat Chieu, with a flying helmet in the crook of an arm stands before MiG-17s with members, including ground crew, of the 921st Fighter Regiment one of whom found the day excessively bright.

On a cool day in the north pilots of the 921st fighter regiment are amused by Le Trong Huyen demonstrating the flying qualities of the MiG-21 with scale models at the request of a photographer. Each, from left to right, Nguyen Ngoc Do, Bui Duc Nhu, Nguyen Duc Thuan and Nguyen Dang Kinh claimed victories. The pilots wear what was known as the Uncle Ho badge; an award given each time a victory was credited.

Pilots of the 923rd Fighter Regiment celebrate receiving a bouquet of flowers from Ho Chi Minh in commemoration of the achievements of the unit in 1966. Holding the basket, left to right, are Le Quang Trung and Nguyen Van Bay. Standing before a MiG-17, left to right, are Vo Van Man, Lou Huy Chao, Tran Huyen, Nguyen Ngoc Phieu, Nguyen Khac Loc, undetermined, and Vu The Xuan.

Pilots of the 923rd Fighter Regiment, from left to right, Ho Van Quy, 3 official victories, Nguyen Ba Dich, 3 official victories, Vo Van Man, 5 official victories and Nguyen Van Bay, 7 official victories, discuss flight operations with the aid of scale models of the MiG-17.

Pilots of the 923rd Fighter Regiment, from left to right, Luu Huy Chao, 6 official victories, Le Hai, 6 official victories, Mai Duc Toai, 2 official victories and Hoang Van Ky, 4 official victories stand before MiG-17F 2039 which Chao was known to have flown in combat.

Pilots of the 923rd Fighter Regiment, left to right, Nguyen Dinh Phuc, 3 official victories and Le Hai, 6 official victories, photographed on 19 November 1967 after engaging aircraft of the USN and having each claimed a F-4 destroyed. Phuc would be shot down and killed on 14 December while Hai would survive the conflict.

Pilots of the 925th Fighter Regiment, from left to right, Nguyen Hong Son, 1 official victory, Nguyen Thang Long, Pham Ngoc Tam, 1 official victory, and Vu Viet Tan discuss aerial maneuvering on 18 May 1972. That day Tam would claim a F-4 destroyed before, along with Long, being forced to eject, fortunately, without injury. Behind is Shenyang J-6 6026 which had often been flown by the original commander of the unit, Le Quang Trung, and was also flown by Son to claim the victory.

Photographed approaching MiG-21 PFM 5057, known to have been flown by Le Thanh Do, on 24 July 1972, are pilots of the 921st Fighter Regiment and the 927th Fighter Regiment, left to right, Bui Thanh Liem, 2 official victories, Nguyen Duc Soat, 6 official victories, Pham Phu Thai, 4 official victories and Ngo Duy Thu, 3 official victories, on 27 June 1972.

Pham Phu Thai attempts to recreate the action for, left to right, Bui Thanh Liem, Nguyen Duc Soat and Ngo Duy Thu each of whom claimed a F-4 destroyed that day. Thai and Liem flew with the 921st Fighter Regiment and Soat and Thu flew with the 927th Fighter Regiment. All four of the aviators survived the conflict.

Nguyen Van Nghia, 5 official victories, describes a battle with hands for the benefit of fellow pilots of the 927th Fighter Regiment, from left to right Nguyen Manh Hai, Nguyen Tuan Viet and Nguyen Van Tho, 1 official victory, which would seem to be a favoured pastime by all. Behind the gesturing pilots may be seen MiG-21s including PFM 5022 and PFM 5015.

Pilots of the 927th Fighter Regiment, left to right, Nguyen Duc Soat, 6 official victories, and Ngo Duy Thu, 3 official victories before a MiG-21.

Ho Chi Minh congratulates Nguyen Van Coc after the pilot was officially credited with a victory; note the Uncle Ho badges worn, one having just been presented by the statesman to the pilot, which was an award given every time a victory was confirmed. The venerated leader of the DRV took great interest in the aerial defence of the nation and often demonstrated appreciation to the members of the Fighter Regiments, not only by the award of the badge, but by the giving of gifts and these presentations, as illustrated, were often made personally. Nguyen Van Coc was awarded more Uncle Ho Badges than any other pilot, as the airman was acknowledged to have despatched 9 aircraft, and was the most successful ace of the American War.

Vo Nguyen Giap, the Minister of Defence, cheerfully engages with pilots of the Fighter Regiments following the Dien Bien Phu in the skies in 1972. The five pilots from right to left are Pham Tuan, who was given credit for the destruction of a B-52 on 27 December 1972, Nguyen Duc Soat, 6 official victories, Do Van Lanh, 4 official victories, Ngo Duy Thu, 3 official victories and Nguyen Hong Nhi, 8 official victories. Giap had prompted the creation of The Air Force Research Committee in 1949 and oversaw the establishment of the Vietnam People's Air Force and the Fighter Regiments within to defend the people of the Democratic Republic of Vietnam from aerial attack.

The Fighter Regiments

921st Red Star Fighter Regiment
Trung đoàn Không quân Tiêm kích 921, Sao Đỏ

The 921st Fighter Regiment was established on 3 February 1964 under the command of Dao Dinh Luyen and was initially equipped with MiG-15UTIs and MiG-17s. Aircraft of the unit were flown from Mengzi in the PRC to Phuc Yen on 6 August. Pilots of the unit first engaged in combat on 3 April 1965 when two F-8s of the USN were claimed destroyed. MiG-21s were made available in November and eventually comprised the complement of aircraft operated by the 921st Fighter Regiment until the conclusion of the American War.

Commanders of the unit served as follows -
Dao Dinh Luyen - 1964-1967
Tran Manh - 1967-1969
Tran Hanh - 1969-1972
Nguyen Ngoc Do - 1972-1974

923rd Hill Of The Peaceful Site Fighter Regiment
Trung đoàn Không quân Tiêm kích 923, Yên Thế

The 923rd Fighter Regiment was established on 7 September 1965 under the command of Nguyen Phuc Trach and was initially equipped with MiG-15UTIs and MiG-17s. To have been based at Kep, for some time all but four of the aircraft were based at Phuc Yen pending improvements at Kep which included the lengthening of the runways so as to reduce the possibility of accidents and the construction of shelters to enable the dispersal of aircraft. Pilots of the unit first engaged in combat on 6 October with F-4s of the USN. MiG-17s and Shenyang J-5s were operated by the unit until the conclusion of the American War.

Commanders of the unit served as follows -
Nguyen Phuc Trach - 1965-1967
Le Oanh - 1968-undetermined

925th Fighter Regiment
Trung đoàn Không quân Tiêm kích 925

The 925th Fighter Regiment was established in February of 1969 under the command of Le Quang Trung and was initially equipped with MiG-15UTIs, perhaps, with MiG-19s, and definitely with Shenyang J-6s, a license built version of the MiG-19 built in the PRC. The unit was based at Kep. An aircraft was lost to friendly fire on 19 January 1972 and pilots of the unit first engaged in combat on 8 May when two F-4s of the USAF were claimed destroyed. The unit may have flown MiG-19s and certainly did fly Shenyang J-6s until the conclusion of the American War.

Commanders of the unit served as follows -
Le Quang Trung - 1969-1970
Mai Duc Toai - 1970-1973

927th Blue Hill Fighter Regiment
Trung đoàn Không quân Tiêm kích 927, Lam Sơn

The 927th Fighter Regiment was established on 3 February 1972 under the command of Nguyen Hong Nhi and was initially equipped with MiG-21s. The unit was formed at Tho Xuan and based at Phuc Yen. Pilots of the unit first engaged in combat on 6 May 1972 when F-4s of the USN were encountered and one MiG-21 was lost. MiG-21s were operated by the unit until the conclusion of the American War.

The Commander of the unit served as follows -
Nguyen Hong Nhi - 1972-1973

The Aces

Pilots known to have registered at least five claims, as individuals or in cooperation with others, are identified by name in anglicized form and Vietnamese form and the number of official victories accredited is noted, thus, pilots who do not meet the generally accepted criteria of having five victories confirmed are included in the listing. The VPAF service of the pilot is described concisely. Known claims of aerial victories, whether subsequently confirmed or not, are listed with the following information: the date of the claim, the aircraft type believed shot down, the unit served with when the claim was made, the aircraft in which the claim was made. Footnotes include information in respect of the aircraft and crew attacked and, or, a listing of pilots who shared the claim.

Bui Duc Nhu

Bùi Đức Nhu

Official Victories: 3

Assigned to the 921st Fighter Regiment, Bui Duc Nhu flew a MiG-21 to claim an AQM-34 destroyed on 6 November 1966 but was forced to eject from a MiG-21 on 2 January 1967 when the unit suffered the loss of five aircraft. Having taken off from Phuc Yen, he and Nguyen Dang Kinh each claimed the destruction of a F-105 laden with bombs in the morning of 3 January 1968. Having amassed combat experience Nhu, who was named a reserve pilot for the flyplast at the memorial service for Ho Chi Minh, was assigned to the 927th Fighter Regiment and would claim the destruction of two F-4s in 1972 while serving with the unit. One was despatched west of Hanoi on 27 June while another was destroyed in proximity to Yen Bai on 5 October. Following that action Nguyen Tien Sam was, fortunately, able shoot down a F-4 pursuing Bui Duc Nhu after which both pilots were able to safely land at Phuc Yen.

Known Claims

06/11/1966   AQM-34   921st F.R.   MiG-21

03/01/1968	F-105[16]	921st F.R.	MiG-21
27/05/1968	AQM-34[17]	921st F.R.	MiG-21
24/06/1972	AQM-34[18]	927th F.R.	MiG-21
27/06/1972	F-4[19]	927th F.R.	MiG-21
05/10/1972	F-4	927th F.R.	MiG-21PFM 5025

Dang Ngoc Ngu

Đặng Ngọc Ngự

Official Victories: 7[20]

Dang Ngoc Ngu was born on 1 November 1939 in Xuan Truong District, Nam Dinh Province and enlisted for military service on 23 March 1959. Selected to be trained at the Krasnador Flight Officer's School in the USSR he there learned, between 1961 and 1966 to fly both the MiG-17 and the MiG-21. Serving with the 921st Fighter Regiment, Ngu flew the MiG-21 and was eventually appointed a flight commander. Credited with the destruction of an AQM-34 on 13 August 1966, on 14 December he claimed a F-105 destroyed. Having damaged a F-105 by cannon fire west of Hanoi on 28 April 1967, when over Hanoi on 22 May Ngu was recognized for the downing of a F-4. Taking off from Phuc Yen on 8 November, with Nguyen Van Ly, he engaged and destroyed a F-4, the tail of which was broken off by a R-3S missile strike. Flying as lead, Ngu took part in an interception on 7

---

[16] Possibly F-105D 58-1157, 469 TFS, 388 TFW, USAF, Colonel James E. Bean, prisoner of war.

[17] A single VPAF claim was made and shared by Bui Duc Nhu and Nguyen Van Lung.

[18] A single VPAF claim was made and shared by Bui Duc Nhu and Le Thanh Dao.

[19] F-4E 67-0243, 308 TFS, 31 TFW attached to 432 Tactical Reconnaissance Wing (TRW), USAF, Captain John P. Cerak (pilot), prisoner of war, Captain David B. Dingee, prisoner of war.

[20] According to Pham Anh Tuyet, of the staff of the Air Defense - Air Force Museum, Hanoi, Dang Ngoc Ngu was credited with 8 official victories.

May 1968 in which the escorting MiG-21s flown by Nguyen Dang Kinh and Nguyen Van Lung were almost attacked in error, but a battle with F-4s ensued resulting in the destruction of a F-4 credited to Nguyen Van Coc, flying as wingman. He survived the harrowing battles through to the end of the Rolling Thunder offensive on 1 November 1968. Ngu was named as a reserve pilot to those designated to conduct a flypast to memorialize Ho Chi Minh following the death of the President of the DRV . Called upon to intercept AQM-34s on reconnaissance missions had been able to destroy one on 24 April and would despatch another on 4 March 1969. With the instigation of Operation Linebacker Ngu was in the thick of the fighting and, on 10 May 1972, despite flying an aircraft with a control surface damaged by a released fuel tank and being under missile fire, was given credit for destroying a F-4 over Kep. On 8 July, having previously flown an uneventful sortie, he took off from Phuc Yen on a subsequent mission, flying MiG-21MF 5118, and, attempting to engage four F-4s, was set upon by a pair of F-4s and shot down and killed by the crew of pilot Richard F. Hardy and WSO Paul T. Lewinski of the USAF who had fired off four AIM-9 and two AIM-7 missiles. Among the most experienced pilots in the VPAF, Dang Ngoc Ngu, having attained the rank of Captain, was posthumously made a Hero Of The Vietnam People's Armed Forces on 11 January 1973.

Known Claims

13/08/1966	AQM-34	921st F.R.	MiG-21
14/12/1966	F-105	921st F.R.	MiG-21
28/04/1967	F-105[21]	921st F.R.	MiG-21
22/05/1967	F-4	921st F.R.	MiG-21
08/11/1967	F-4[22]	921st F.R.	MiG-21
24/04/1968	AQM-34	921st F.R.	MiG-21
04/03/1969	AQM-34	921st F.R.	MiG-21
10/05/1972	F-4	921st F.R.	MiG-21MF 5136

[21] F-105 airframe number undetermined, 44 TFS, 388 TFW, damaged, aircrew undetermined.

[22] F-4D 66-0250, 555 TFS, 8 TFW, USAF, Major William S. Gordon (pilot), recovered, First Lieutenant Richard C. Brenneman, prisoner of war.

Dinh Ton

Đinh Tôn

Official Victories: 4

Born on 5 September 1936, Dinh Ton joined the armed forces in December 1952. He travelled to the CR to commence pilot training in 1957. Returning to the DRV in 1958, Ton became a member of the 910th Air Training Regiment until 1961 when service began with the 919th Air Transport Regiment flying the Li-2. He began to train on the MiG-21 in the USSR in 1965 following which came a return to the DRV in order to join the 921st Fighter Regiment.   Flying the MiG-21F-13 Ton was credited with the destruction of three AQM-34s, one in cooperation with Tran Viet, in the spring of 1968.   With Nguyen Tien Sam he engaged USN F-4s of VF-102 flying from USS America on 16 June and fired a R-3S missile which exploded in the tailpipe of the target resulting in the death of the RIO Bernard F. Rupinski and the capture of pilot Walter E. Wilber following which leave was obtained to marry Tran Thi Dien Hong on 27 July.   Ton participated in the effort to interfere with American aircraft flying over supply routes of the VPA in the spring of 1971. Great coordination between ground control and pilot was required to be able to engage such a target travelling at low altitude and low speed but with capable assistance he was able to claim two victories, an O-2 on 13 April and an OV-10 on 20 April.   Ton endeavoured to intercept B-52s in the darkness of 4 October after taking off from the airbase at Dong Hoi but radar was made ineffective by electronic countermeasures.   Nonetheless, he spotted two lit B-52s flying at 9000 metres (29,527 feet) and attempted an interception but was thwarted when the lights seen were extinguished and F-4s interfered.   On 11 September 1972 Ton was flying with Vasilij Motlov in a MiG-21 U type practicing manoeuvres when ground control gave warning that enemy aircraft were flying within close proximity.   He and the Soviet instructor had only 800 litres (211 gallons) of fuel left aboard the aircraft when the engagement began.   Several AAMs were avoided but the fuel was consumed in the effort and the two pilots were forced to eject following which the aircraft was struck. Dinh Ton was made a Hero of the Vietnam People's Armed Forces on 31 December 1973 and would rise to the rank of Senior Colonel before succumbing to cancer in 1980.

Known Claims			
15/04/1968	AQM-34	921st F.R.	MiG-21F-13
26/05/1968	AQM-34	921st F.R.	MiG-21F-13
02/06/1968	AQM-34[23]	921st F.R.	MiG-21F-13
16/06/1968	F-4[24]	921st F.R.	MiG-21
13/04/1971	O-2	921st F.R.	MiG-21
20/04/1971	OV-10	921st F.R.	MiG-21

Do Van Lanh

Đỗ Văn Lanh

Official Victories: 4

Do Van Lanh was born on 21 October 1948 in Ninh Binh Province and enlisted in the armed forces in August 1965. He learned to fly the MiG-17 in the PRC between 1965 and 1968 and served with the 923rd Fighter Regiment following which began instruction on the MiG-21 and service with the 921st Fighter Regiment. On 20 May 1972 Lanh took off from Phuc Yen to accompany Luong The Phuc on a sortie during which some 12 F-4s were encountered. Having avoided an AAM, he fired two R-3S missiles in succession, one of which struck the F-4 of John D. Markle, who had claimed a MiG-21 destroyed days before, on 10 May, and James W. Williams and thus forced the ejection of the crew. Having safely undertaken a landing without fuel on 24 May, Lanh made a claim for a F-4 destroyed on 13 June and 21 June again attacked F-4s, which were to drop chaff, and duly destroyed one. He and Bui Thanh Liem pursued and together were credited with the destruction of an AQM-34 on 24 June. On 9 September Lanh, when again flying with Luong The Phuc, encountered F-4s and the

---

[23] A single VPAF claim was made and shared by Dinh Ton and Tran Viet.

[24] F-4J 155548, VF-102, USN, USS America, Commander Walter E. Wilber (pilot), prisoner of war, Lieutenant (Junior Grade) Bernard F. Rupinski, killed in action.

latter fired a missile believed to have caused damage before the former fired a missile which ultimately caused the crew of the target to eject. Phuc was shot down when trying to land all but out of fuel, being fortunate to survive the necessary ejection, but Lanh was able to land safely. The following day he and Nguyen Cong Huy provided cover for a brace of Ilyushin IL-28s returning to Phuc Yen after having bombed LS-32, a landing strip used to assist covert operations undertaken by American forces at Bouam Long in the KL. Lanh survived a harrowing battle on 27 December when flying with courage and patience as a target for a F-4 which was stalked and claimed destroyed by Duong Ba Khang of the 927th Fighter Regiment. He was made a Hero of the Vietnam People's Armed Forces on 11 January 1973. Do Van Lanh, a pilot much respected in the service, who, in 1975 had married Nguyen Thi Lam and had children, achieved the rank of Lieutenant Colonel but was to die in a flying accident when attempting to land through inclement weather on 9 July 1980.

Known Claims			
20/05/1972	F-4[25]	921st F.R.	MiG-21
13/06/1972	F-4	921st F.R.	MiG-21
21/06/1972	F-4[26]	921st F.R.	MiG-21MF 5128
24/06/1972	AQM-34[27]	921st F.R.	MiG-21
09/09/1972	F-4[28]	921st F.R.	MiG-21MF 5108

---

[25] F-4D 65-0600, 555 TFS, 432 TRW, USAF, First Lieutenant John D. Markle, recovered, Captain James W. Williams, prisoner of war.

[26] F-4E 69-0282, 334 TFS, 4 TFW attached to 8 TFW, USAF, Captain George A. Rose (pilot), prisoner of war, First Lieutenant Peter A. Callaghan, prisoner of war.

[27] A single VPAF claim was made and shared by Bui Thanh Liem and Do Van Lanh.

[28] F4E 69-7565, 307 TFS, 31 TFW attached to 432 TRW, USAF, Captain William J. Dalecky (pilot), recovered, Captain Terry M. Murphy, recovered. A single VPAF claim was made and shared by Do Van Lanh and Luong The Phuc.

Dong Van Song

Đồng Văn Song

Official Victories: 4

Born on 2 August 1940, Dong Van Song joined the armed forces in 1961. He trained to pilot the MiG-21 in the USSR between 1962 and 1965 and became a member of the 921st Fighter Regiment in 1965 with which MiG-21PFL 4127, which was camouflaged, was flown. Flying with Nguyen Dang Kinh, Song participated in the aerial combat debut of the MiG-21 in VPAF service when F-4s were engaged on 23 April 1966. When trying to intercept EB-66s on 26 April he was unable to prevent the loss of the MiG-21 flown by Nguyen Hong Nhi when the two were engaged by F-4s. On 11 July Song and Vu Ngoc Dinh, in action with MiG-17s of the 923rd Fighter Regiment, were credited with the destruction of a F-105 that, apparently, ran out of fuel as a result of the combat. On 5 November he and Bui Dinh Kinh were attempting to intercept an EB-66 when both were attacked by F-4s and forced to eject. Song and Le Trong Huyen cooperated to claim a F-105 sent down over Van Yen on 12 May 1967, the USAF acknowledging the loss of Captain Earl W. Grenzebach, who was born in Canada, in the vicinity and they did so again to claim an A-4 sent down over Hai Duong on 11 July though the USN recorded no such loss. Often in combat, he was forced to eject on 10 August and 24 October but, claims were made for a F-4, when flying with Nguyen Hong Nhi, on 26 September and on 14 January 1968 with Nguyen Dang Kinh for an EB-66 which, struck in the starboard engine by a R-3S missile, crashed in a mountainous area of the DRV bordering the KL. Dong Van Song was to be made a Hero of the Vietnam People's Armed Forces and would ultimately attain the rank of Senior Colonel.

Known Claims

11/07/1966	F-105[29]	921st F.R.	MiG-21

---

[29] F-105D 61-0121, 355 TFW, 34 TFS, USAF, Major William L. McClelland, recovered. A single VPAF claim was made and shared by Dong Van Song and Vu Ngoc Dinh.

12/05/1967	F-105[30]	921st F.R.	MiG-21
11/07/1967	A-4[31]	921st F.R.	MiG-21
26/09/1967	F-4[32]	921st F.R.	MiG-21
14/01/1968	EB-66[33]	921st F.R.	MiG-21

Duong Trung Tan

Dương Trung Tân

Official Victories: 2

Trained to fly the MiG-17, Duong Trung Tan was assigned to the 923rd Fighter Regiment. Though he was forced to eject while in combat with USN aircraft on 21 June 1966 the credit for the Vought RF-8 Crusader and F-8 claimed destroyed was shared by all members of the flight engaged. Tan recorded victories on 19 April 1967 over a F-105 and an A-1 while USAF aircraft undertook a SAR operation. Following a sortie on 12 May he asserted that two F-105s had been despatched in cooperation with Nguyen Van Tho. October proved an eventful month for Tan who made a claim for an A-4, on the fifth and was made to eject when engaged with F-4s on the 26th of the month. He was assigned to the 925th Fighter Regiment but was to die in a crash after taking off in a MiG-19 on 13 September 1969. Duong Trung Tan attained the rank of Senior Lieutenant and was made a

---

[30] Possibly F-105D 59-1728, 357 TFS, 355 TFW, USAF, Captain Earl W. Grenzebach, killed in action. A single VPAF claim was made and shared by Dong Van Song and Le Trong Huyen.

[31] A single VPAF claim was made and shared by Dong Van Song and Le Trong Huyen.

[32] A single VPAF claim was made and shared by Dong Van Song and Nguyen Hong Nhi.

[33] EB-66C 55-0388, 41 Tactical Electronic Warfare Squadron (TEWS), 355 TFW, USAF, Major Pollard H. Mercer (pilot), recovered, died of wounds 20/1/1968, Major Thomas W. Sumpter, prisoner of war, Major Irby D. Terrell, prisoner of war, Captain Hubert C. Walker, prisoner of war, First Lieutenant Ronald M. Lebert, prisoner of war, First Lieutenant Attilio Pedroli, recovered, First Lieutenant James E. Thompson, recovered. A single VPAF claim was made and shared by Dong Van Song and Nguyen Dang Kinh.

Hero of the Vietnam People's Armed Forces in recognition of service to the DRV.

Known Claims

21/06/1966	1 RF-8,			
	1 F-8[34]	923rd F.R.	MiG-17	
19/04/1967	1 F-105,			
	1 A-1	923rd F.R.	MiG-17	
12/05/1967	F-105	923rd F.R.	MiG-17	
05/10/1967	A-4	923rd F.R.	MiG-17	

Hoang Van Ky

Hoàng Văn Kỷ

Official Victories: 4

Hoang Van Ky was born in 1939 and enlisted for military service in March 1959. Trained to fly the MiG-17 in the USSR between 1962 and 1965, he was assigned to the 921st Fighter Regiment. After being transferred to the 923rd Fighter Regiment, Ky, who was known to fly both MiG-17F 2076 and MiG-17F 2431, claimed an initial victory on 20 September 1966 and, recognized for destroying a F-4 on 5 February 1967, was given credit, with the other members of the flight engaged, for the downing of a F-105 on the 24 April and on the following day as well. Having claimed a F-4 shot down on 4 May, on 12 May he and fellow flight members, as well as anti-aircraft units, were acknowledged as having destroyed three F-4s. Serving at the rank of Senior Lieutenant, Hoang Van Ky was killed when in combat over Vinh Phuc on 5 June with F-4s of the USAF, as were Tran Huyen and Truong Van Cung, during a period of time when many sorties were flown and significant losses were incurred by the 923rd Fighter Regiment but

---

[34] One of the claims was possibly RF-8A 146830, Detachment L, Navy Light Photographic Squadron (VFP)-63, USN, USS Hancock, Lieutenant Leonard C. Eastman, prisoner of war. One of the claims was F-8E 149152, VF-211, USN, USS Hancock, Lieutenant Commander Cole Black, prisoner of war. Two VPAF claims were made and shared by Duong Trung Tan, Nguyen Van Bay, Pham Thanh Chung, Phan Van Tuc.

would be acknowledged, posthumously, as a Hero of the Vietnam People's Armed Forces on 28 April 2000.

Known Claims			
20/09/1966	F-105	923rd F.R.	MiG-17
05/02/1967	F-4	923rd F.R.	MiG-17F 2431
24/04/1967	F-105[35]	923rd F.R.	MiG-17
25/04/1967	F-105[36]	923rd F.R.	MiG-17
04/05/1967	F-4	923rd F.R	MiG-17
12/05/1967	3 F-4s[37]	923rd F.R.	MiG-17

Le Hai
Lê Hải
Official Victories: 6

Born on 29 April 1942 in Mo Duc District, Quang Ngai Province, Le Hai joined the armed forces on 21 July 1961. He received flight training with the 910th Training Regiment in the DRV from 1961 through 1965 before being assigned to the 923rd Fighter Regiment. In 1967 Hai flew as a member of a flight which claimed a victory over a F-105 on both 24 April and 25 April, recognition for which was given to all, and, days later on 28 April, another such combat took place resulting in the destruction of a F-105 credited to

[35] A single VPAF claim was made and shared by Hoang Van Ky, Le Hai, Luu Huy Chao, Mai Duc Toai.

[36] F-105D 62-4294, 354 TFS, 355 TFW, USAF, First Lieutenant Robert L. Weskamp, killed in action. A single VPAF claim was made and shared by Hoang Van Ky, Le Hai, Luu Huy Chao, Mai Duc Toai.

[37] One of the claims was F-4C 63-7614, 390 TFS, 366 TFW, USAF, Colonel Norman C. Gaddis (pilot), prisoner of war, First Lieutenant James M. Jefferson, killed in action. One or both of the other claims may have been F-105D 59-1728, 357 TFS, 355 TFW, USAF, Captain Earl W. Grenzebach Jr., killed in action and, or, F-105F 63-8269 34 TFS, 388 TFW, USAF, Captain Peter P. Pitman (pilot), killed in action, Captain Robert A. Stewart, killed in action. Three VPAF claims were made and shared by Cao Than Thinh, Hoang Van Ky, Le Hai, Ngo Duc Mai and anti-aircraft units.

the flight engaged which included Hai. He was one of several VPAF members personally decorated by Ho Chi Minh in the spring. Hai was among a flight of pilots who all were given credit, in cooperation with anti aircraft units, for downing three F-4s over Hoa Lac on 12 May when the Ha Dong Barracks were a target, but the month was particularly arduous for the 923rd Fighter Regiment as losses of equipment and men resulted in limited capability through the summer. Reinforcement with aircraft and pilots enabled an increase of operations come the autumn and he was given credit for the destruction of a F-4 on 19 November, following the failure of the radio in the aircraft flown by Ho Van Quy, when assuming the lead of a flight engaging USN aircraft. Flying MiG-17F 2044, Hai participated in an interception on 17 December involving several pilots of the 923rd Fighter Regiment as well as members of Group Z and was noted to have damaged, but not destroyed, a F-4. Frequently in combat, he was recognized for having despatched two aircraft in the summer of 1968; a F-4 on 14 June and, in cooperation with Luu Huy Chao, a F-8 on 29 July both of which were thought to have crashed in the Gulf of Tonkin. Following the cessation of Rolling Thunder, Hai sortied against reconnaissance drones and, flying with Hoang Cong, was credited with an AQM-34 destroyed on 3 August 1969. A final victory was claimed on 6 March 1972 when engaging F-4s, thought to have been of the USN, and one was set afire and believed destroyed following which he continued in the attack until running out of ammunition. Having been made a Hero Of The Vietnam People's Armed Forces on 25 August 1970, Le Hai would ultimately rise to the rank of Senior Colonel.

Known Claims

24/04/1967	F-105[38]	923rd F.R.	MiG-17
25/04/1967	F-105[39]	923rd F.R.	MiG-17
28/04/1967	F-105	923rd F.R.	MiG-17

---

[38] A single VPAF claim was made and shared by Hoang Van Ky, Le Hai, Luu Huy Chao, Mai Duc Toai.

[39] F-105D 62-4294, 354 TFS, 355 TFW, USAF, First Lieutenant Robert L. Weskamp, killed in action. A single VPAF claim was made and shared by Hoang Van Ky, Le Hai, Luu Huy Chao, Mai Duc Toai.

12/05/1967	3 F-4s[40]	923rd F.R.	MiG-17
19/11/1967	F-4[41]	923rd F.R.	Shenyang J-5 2055
14/06/1968	F-4	923rd F.R.	Shenyang J-5 3020
29/07/1968	F-8[42]	923rd F.R.	MiG-17
03/08/1969	AQM-34[43]	923rd F.R.	Shenyang J-5 3020
06/03/1972	F-4	923rd F.R.	MiG-17

Le Quang Trung

Lê Quang Trung

Official Victories: 5

Le Quang Trung was born in 1934 and enlisted for military service in May 1949 then earning a reputation for ardent patriotism. He began pilot training in the PRC in 1956 which was completed in 1964 and by then was capable of flying the MiG-17. Originally a member of the 921st Fighter Regiment, Trung was later transferred to the 923rd Fighter Regiment. Having begun flying on operations in 1965, he was credited with an initial victory in the afternoon of 12 June 1966, after taking off from Kep with Vo Van Man, when a F-8 was reported destroyed. Victories over F-105s were claimed on 17 August and 20 September. Engaged against A-1s and F-8s on

---

[40] One of the claims was F-4C 63-7614, 390 TFS, 366 TFW, USAF, Colonel Norman C. Gaddis (pilot), prisoner of war, First Lieutenant James M. Jefferson, killed in action. One or both of the other claims may have been F-105D 59-1728, 357 TFS, 355 TFW, USAF, Captain Earl W. Grenzebach Jr., killed in action and, or, F-105F 63-8269 34 TFS, 388 TFW, USAF, Captain Peter P. Pitman (pilot), killed in action, Captain Robert A. Stewart, killed in action. Three VPAF claims were made and shared by Cao Than Thinh, Hoang Van Ky, Le Hai, Ngo Duc Mai and anti-aircraft units.

[41] F-4B 150997, VF-151, USN, USS Coral Sea, Lieutenant Commander Claude D. Clower (pilot), prisoner of war, Lieutenant (Junior Grade) Walter O. Estes, killed in action.

[42] A single VPAF claim was made and shared by Le Hai and Luu Huy Chao.

[43] A single VPAF claim was made and shared by Hoang Cong and Le Hai.

9 October Trung was able to claim one of the former destroyed and escape from the latter. In combat with F-105s which had been bombing the Yen Vien railway yards on 4 December he registered one as destroyed though fellow flight member Luu Duc Sy was subsequently killed in the battle. 25 April 1967 was a day of much combat and several claims were made including one over a F-105 by Trung. He undertook training on the MiG-19, in the DRV, and was transferred to the 925th Fighter Regiment as the commanding officer of the unit in 1969, often flying J-6 6026, but was to die in a mid air collision with Bui Dinh Doan on 6 April 1970. Le Quang Trung, serving at the rank of Major when killed, would posthumously be made a Hero of the Vietnam People's Armed Forces on 20 December 1994.

Known Claims

12/06/1966	F-8	923rd F.R.	MiG-17
17/08/1966	F-105[44]	923rd F.R.	MiG-17F 2072
20/09/1966	F-105	923rd F.R.	MiG-17
09/10/1966	A-1	923rd F.R.	MiG-17
04/12/1966	F-105	923rd F.R.	MiG-17
25/04/1967	F-105	923rd F.R.	MiG-17

Le Thanh Dao

Lê Thanh Đạo

Official Victories: 6

Born on 20 September 1944 in Tu Liem District, Hanoi, Le Thanh Dao joined the military on 5 July 1963, and trained in the USSR to fly the MiG-21 between 1965 and 1968. He served with the 921st Fighter Regiment, participating in the memorial flight for Ho Chi Minh on 9 September 1969, claiming victories over an OV-10 in cooperation with Mai Van Cuong on 10 May 1971 and on 18 December while flying with Vo Si Giap, when a F-4 flying as cover for the extraction of a CIA combat team in the KL near the border with the DRV was destroyed. Having become a member of the

[44] Possibly F-105F 63-8308, 354 TFS, 355 TFW, USAF, Major Joseph W. Brand (pilot), killed in action, Major Donald M. Singer, killed in action.

927th Fighter Regiment, Dao was directed by flight controller Le Than Chon on 10 May 1972, a day of intense fighting, to claim the first victory of the unit, over a F-4, while flying MiG-21PFM 5040, in the company of Vu Van Hop who subsequently claimed a victory during the interception as well. On 11 September he engaged a F-4, sent to drop chaff to confuse radar systems operators, destroying the target with a R-3S missile, and another F-4 was claimed as shot down on 1 October. During a combat on 15 October cannon fire from a F-4 flown by the crew of Gary M. Rubus and WSO James L. Hendrickson struck the MiG-21 flown by Dao. Forced to eject he was subjected to an attack while descending by parachute and, with many holes in the canopy, struck the ground with enough force to break both legs and vertebra while sustaining head injury as well before being retrieved by civilians then transported by a Mi-6 to a hospital to begin a prolonged period of recovery. Le Thanh Dao was made a Hero Of The Vietnam People's Armed Forces on 11 January 1973 and would attain the rank of Senior Colonel prior to retiring from service in 2006.

Known Claims

10/05/1971	OV-10[45]	921st F.R.	MiG-21
18/12/1971	F-4[46]	921st F.R.	MiG-21PFM 5032
10/05/1972	F-4[47]	927th F.R.	MiG-21PFM 5040
12/06/1972	F-4	927th F.R.	MiG-21
24/06/1972	AQM-34[48]	927th F.R.	MiG-21

---

[45] A single VPAF claim was made and shared by Le Thanh Dao and Mai Van Cuong.

[46] F-4D 66-0241, 555 TFS, 432 TRW, USAF, Major Kenneth R. Johnson (pilot), prisoner of war, First Lieutenant Samuel R. Vaughan, prisoner of war.

[47] F-4J 155797, VF-92, USN, USS Constellation, Commander Harry L. Blackburn Jr. (pilot), killed in action or died date unknown, Lieutenant Stephen A. Rudloff, prisoner of war.

[48] A single VPAF claim was made and shared by Bui Duc Nhu and Le Thanh Dao.

24/07/1972	F-4[49]	927th F.R.	MiG-21PFM 5057
09/091972	F-4	927th F.R.	MiG-21
11/09/1972	F-4[50]	927th F.R.	MiG-21PFM 5017
01/10/1972	F-4	927th F.R.	MiG-21

Le Trong Huyen
Lê Trọng Huyên
Official Victories: 4

Trained to fly the MiG-17 in the PRC between 1960 and 1964, Le Trong Huyen, having been born in 1934, became an operational pilot at some 30 years of age, flying the aircraft with the 921st Fighter Regiment before learning to fly the MiG-21 in Vietnam. A first victory was gained when flying the type on 21 September 1966 and destroying a F-105 with a R-3S missile fired from extreme range. After being engaged in a battle of manoeuvre with a F-105 on 2 December he was credited with a victory. Directed by ground control, on 30 April 1967, Huyen and Vu Ngoc Dinh attacked a pair F-105s that had been supporting a SAR operation, and were about to leave the combat area to refuel, and each claimed a victory one of which was shot down while the other was damaged but able to escape and effect a safe landing. He flew with Dong Van Song on more than one occasion and the pair of MiG-21 pilots twice claimed victories together; a F-105 on 12 May and an A-4 on 11 July. Huyen, having risen to the rank of Major, was to die on 3 March 1972 when flying, as a passenger, in a Li-2 that was shot down in the vicinity of Vinh by a S-75 launched in in error, but, years of service and accomplishment would be publicly recognized posthumously with the award of the title Hero of the Vietnamese People's Armed Forces on 28 April 2000.

[49] Possibly F-4E 66-0369, 421 TFS, 366 TFW, USAF, Captain Samuel A. Hodnett (pilot), recovered, First Lieutenant David M. Fallert, recovered.

[50] F-4E 69-0288, 335 TFS, 4 TFW attached to 8 TFW, USAF, Captain Brian M. Ratzlaff (pilot), prisoner of war, Captain Jerome D. Heeren, prisoner of war.

Known Claims

21/09/1966	F-105[51]	921st F.R.	MiG-21PFL 4221
02/12/1966	F-105[52]	921st F.R.	MiG-21
30/04/1967	F-105[53]	921st F.R.	MiG-21PFL 4324
12/05/1967	F-105[54]	921st F.R.	MiG-21
11/07/1967	A-4[55]	921st F.R.	MiG-21

Luu Huy Chao

Lưu Huy Chao

Official Victories: 6

Lu Huy Chao was born in Dong Son District, Thanh Hoah Province, on 22 December 1936 and, having graduated from high school, enlisted in the armed forces on 12 February 1954 to defend the DRV from the military of the FR. He went, in 1960, to the PRC to train to be a pilot, returning to the DRV in 1962. After another stint of training in the PRC between 1963 and 1965, Chao entered service with the 923rd Fighter Regiment claiming a Douglas C-47 Skytrain destroyed on 17 April 1966 and a F-4 on 26 April. Directed toward F-105s flying at an altitude of less than 1000 metres (3,280 feet) on 12 August he was able to destroy one and then dive away, apparently, without being seen by any of the American pilots.   Chao

---

[51] F-105D 62-4371, 357 TFS, 355 TFW, USAF, Captain Glendon L. Ammon, killed in action.

[52] F-105D 59-1820, 34 TFS, 388 TFW, USAF, Captain Monte L. Moorberg, killed in action.

[53] Either F-105D 61-0130, 333 TFS, 355 TFW, USAF, Captain Joseph S. Abbott, prisoner of war or F-105 airframe number undetermined, damaged, Major Albert J. Lenski, 333 TFS, 355 TFW, USAF.

[54] Possibly F-105D 59-1728, 357 TFS, 355 TFW, USAF, Captain Earl W. Grenzebach, killed in action. A single VPAF claim was made and shared by Dong Van Song and Le Trong Huyen.

[55] A single VPAF claim was made and shared by Dong Van Song and Le Trong Huyen.

participated in the aerial battles over Hanoi in April 1967 and shared claims over F-105s on the 24th and on the 25th of the month with other pilots of the 923rd Fighter Regiment. Made a flight commander, in the spring, he was among the pilots decorated by Ho Chi Minh. During an intense battle with F-8s on 14 December Chao was able to force one pursuing Le Hai away and shoot down another when supported by Nguyen Dinh Phuc who was killed. Engaging F-4s on 17 December he managed to destroy one, as did Bui Van Suu, though Nguyen Hong Thai was killed in the action. Returning to Gia Lam following an, until then, uneventful sortie on 3 January 1968 a flight of MiG-17s of the 923rd Fighter Regiment encountered eight F-4s and during the ensuing combat, in which a F-4 was claimed destroyed in cooperation with Bui Van Suu, the MiG-17 flown by Chao was damaged by a missile and it was deemed necessary to leave the battle and land at Phuc Yen. On 14 June 1968, between 1430 hours and 1500 hours, he and Le Hai, flying from Gia Lam, each claimed a F-4 sent down and the two pilots would together claim a F-8 destroyed on 29 July as well. Made a Hero Of The Vietnam People's Armed Forces on 22 December 1969, Luu Huy Chao served as the deputy commander of the 923rd Fighter Regiment, rising to the rank of Senior Colonel, and, after retiring from service, wrote a memoir of life during the American War, We And The MiG-17, before dying in 2014.

Known Claims

17/04/1966	C-47	923rd F.R.	MiG-17
26/04/1966	F-4	923rd F.R.	MiG-17
12/08/1966	F-105[56]	923rd F.R.	MiG-17
24/04/1967	F-105[57]	923rd F.R.	MiG-17F 2039
25/04/1967	F-105[58]	923rd F.R.	MiG-17

---

[56] F-105D 61-0156, 333 TFS, 355 TFW, USAF, Captain David J. Allinson, killed in action.

[57] A single VPAF claim was made and shared by Hoang Van Ky, Le Hai, Luu Huy Chao, Mai Duc Toai.

[58] F-105D 62-4294, 354 TFS, 355 TFW, USAF, Captain Robert L. Weskamp, killed in action. A single VPAF claim was made and shared by Hoang Van Ky, Le Hai, Luu Huy Chao, Mai Duc Toai.

14/12/1967	F-8[59]	923rd F.R.	Shenyang J-5 2011
17/12/1967	F-4[60]	923rd F.R.	MiG-17F 2039
03/01/1968	F-4[61]	923rd F.R.	MiG-17
14/06/1968	F-4	923rd F.R.	MiG-17
29/07/1968	F-8[62]	923rd F.R.	MiG-17

Mai Van Cuong

Mai Văn Cương

Official Victories: 8

Born on 2 February 1941 in Hoang Hoa District, Thanh Hoa Province, Mai Van Cuong joined the military on 28 March 1959. He began pilot training, in 1961, learning to fly the MiG-17 in the USSR. Back to the DRV in 1964, Cuong served with the 921st Fighter Regiment but again travelled to the USSR, in 1965, to train on the MiG-21. He returned to the DRV in 1966 and was given credit for sending down a F-105 on 8 October. On 6 January 1967 Cuong ejected to escape from MiG-21PFL 4023 which was struck by an AIM-7 missile and on 26 October would survive the destruction of the MiG-21 flown by ejecting when being engaged, by the crew of pilot Robert P. Hickey and RIO Jeremy G. Morris, during a convoluted combat with F-4s of the USN. Flying in the company of Dang Ngoc Nhu on 28 April, he encountered two F-105s returning from an AAA suppression mission; Nhu damaging one with cannon while Cuong destroyed one using both cannon and missile. He made two victory claims in the autumn, a F-105 on 30 September and a F-4 on 7 October and, having destroyed an AQM-34 on 16

---

[59] A single VPAF claim was made and shared by Luu Huy Chao and Nguyen Dinh Phuc.

[60] Possibly F-4D 66-7774, 497 TFS, 8 TFW, USAF, Major Kenneth R. Fleenor (pilot), prisoner of war, First Lieutenant Terry L. Boyer, prisoner of war.

[61] A single VPAF claim was made and shared by Bui Van Suu and Luu Huy Chao.

[62] A single VPAF claim was made and shared by Le Hai and Luu Huy Chao.

May, he subsequently became proficient at stalking and despatching reconnaissance drones. Cuong was selected to participate in the memorial flypast for Ho Chi Minh on 9 September 1969 leading the 3rd Flight over Ba Dinh Square. Mai Van Cuong, was made a Hero Of The Vietnam People's Armed Forces on 22 December 1969, claimed an OV-10 destroyed, in collaboration with Le Thanh Dao, on 10 May 1971 and ultimately attained the rank of Major General.

Known Claims

08/10/1966	F-105	921st F.R.	MiG-21
28/04/1967	F-105[63]	921st F.R.	MiG-21PFL
16/05/1967	AQM-34	921st F.R.	MiG-21
30/09/1967	F-105	921st F.R.	MiG-21
07/10/1967	F-4[64]	921st F.R.	MiG-21
19/06/1968	AQM-34	921st F.R.	MiG-21
03/09/1968	AQM-34	921st F.R.	MiG-21
20/09/1968	AQM-34	921st F.R.	MiG-21
09/02/1969	AQM-34	921st F.R.	MiG-21
24/06/1969	AQM-34	921st F.R.	MiG-21
10/05/1971	OV-10[65]	921st F.R.	MiG-21

Ngo Duc Mai

Ngô Đức Mai
Official Victories: 3

Ngo Duc Mai was born on 6 November 1938 in Hung Nguyen District, Nghe An Province and, having become, in 1955, a member of the military, was

---

[63] F-105D 58-1151, 44 TFS, 388 TFW, USAF, Captain Franklin A. Caras, killed in action.

[64] Possibly F-4D 65-0727, 555 TFS, 8 TFW, USAF, Major Ivan D. Appleby (pilot), killed in action, Captain William R. Austin, prisoner of war.

[65] A single VPAF claim was made and shared by Le Thanh Dao and Mai Van Cuong.

selected for training in the PRC and commenced the program in 1960. As a member of the 923rd Fighter Regiment he participated in the combat debut of the unit on 4 March 1966 claiming a F-4 destroyed after having closed in to within 200 metres (656 feet) of the target following which an emergency landing was made when the MiG-17 flown was all but out of fuel. On 14 July the 923rd Fighter Regiment intercepted a USN attack upon storage depots by Nam Dinh and Mai was able to so damage a F-8, that the pilot, Richard M. Bellinger, the commanding officer of VF-162, was forced to eject, due to a damaged hydraulic system, to be retrieved by the USAF. He was frequently to be in action and was to amass significant experience of aerial combat. Following an interception of a strike on Ha Dong on 12 May 1967 Mai was one of four pilots to share credit for the claim of three F-4s shot down with anti aircraft units though it may have been that F-105s were engaged as well. He took part in many of the battles through the spring which proved so costly to the 923rd Fighter Regiment including that of 3 June over Bac Giang. Flying one of three MiG-17s shot down, Ngo Duc Mai was killed but would be made a Hero of the Vietnam People's Armed Forces on 30 August 1995.

Known Claims

04/03/1966	F-4	923rd F.R.	MiG-17
14/07/1966	F-8[66]	923rd F.R.	MiG-17
12/05/1967	3 F-4s[67]	923rd F.R.	Shenyang J-5 2011

---

[66] F-8E 150908, VF-162, USN, USS Oriskany, Commander Richard M. Bellinger, recovered.

[67] One of the claims was F-4C 63-7614, 390 TFS, 366 TFW, USAF, Colonel Norman C. Gaddis (pilot), prisoner of war, First Lieutenant James M. Jefferson, killed in action. One or both of the other claims may have been F-105D 59-1728, 357 TFS, 355 TFW, USAF, Captain Earl W. Grenzebach Jr., killed in action and, or, F-105F 63-8269 34 TFS, 388 TFW, USAF, Captain Peter P. Pitman (pilot), killed in action, Captain Robert A. Stewart, killed in action. Three VPAF claims were made and shared by Cao Than Thinh, Hoang Van Ky, Le Hai, Ngo Duc Mai and anti-aircraft units.

Nguyen Ba Dich
Nguyễn Bá Địch
Official Victories: 3

Flying the MiG-17 with the 923rd Fighter Regiment during the spring of 1967, Nguyen Ba Dich fought in several intense combats against both the USAF and the USN. Taking off from Gia Lam, he claimed a victory on 19 April over a F-105 participating in an attack on military barracks at Xuan Mai thus instigating a SAR mission which resulted in the loss of an A-1 and ultimately failed. Part of an element that flew to operate from Kien An on 23 April, on 24 April, after the group took to the air, he was able to spot aircraft some 10 kilometres (6.2 miles) away which led to the interception of USN F-4s of VF 114 flying from USS Kitty Hawk during which the pilots of the 923rd Fighter Regiment cooperated to claim two destroyed and thereafter all landed safely at Gia Lam before returning to Kien An. On the 25 April another attack was made upon USN aircraft and Dich flew with a flight which was credited with the destruction of 2 A-4s and a F-8. He participated in several sorties in the following days and was in action against F-4s on 1 May, claiming one shot down only to be killed thereafter. Nguyen Ba Dich, 30 years old at death, who had married Pham Thi Nu and was serving as a Lieutenant would, on 30 January 2011, be recognized as a Hero of the Vietnam People's Armed Forces.

Known Claims

Date	Claim	Unit	Aircraft
19/04/1967	F-105[68]	923rd F.R.	MiG-17
24/04/1967	2 F-4s[69]	923rd F.R.	MiG-17
25/04/1967	2 A-4s,		

[68] F-105F 63-8341, 357 TFS, 355 TFW, USAF, Major Thomas M. Madison (pilot), prisoner of war, Major Thomas J. Sterling, prisoner of war.

[69] One of the claims was F-4B 153000, VF-114, USN, USS Kitty Hawk, Lieutenant Commander Charles E. Southwick (pilot), recovered, Ensign James W. Laing, recovered. Two VPAF claims were made and shared by Nguyen Ba Dich, Nguyen The Hon, Nguyen Van Bay, Vo Van Man.

	1 F-8[70]	923rd F.R.	MiG-17
01/05/1967	F-4	923rd F.R.	MiG-17

Nguyen Dang Kinh

Nguyễn Đăng Kỉnh

Official Victories: 6

Born on 19 August 1941 in Xuan Truong District, Nam Dinh Province, by the Red River, Nguyen Dang Kinh enlisted in the armed forces on 23 March 1959 and was trained to fly the MiG-17 and MiG-21 in the USSR between 1961 and 1965. Serving with the 921st Fighter Regiment, he was forced to eject at a height of 200 metres (656 feet) after MiG-21PFL 4121 suffered hydraulic system damage in combat with F-4s of the USAF on 23 April 1966. Kinh claimed an AQM-34 destroyed on 21 July. When flying with Bui Duc Nhu on 5 December he was credited with shooting down a F-105. On 2 January 1967 two flights of four aircraft were ordered into the air from Phuc Yen, despite dense cloud over the airbase. Emerging into sunlight one by one, the MiG-21s were set upon by F-4s of the 8th TFW led by Robin Olds. Kinh, flying MiG-21PFL 4126, was one of the first flight into the air from which all of the pilots were forced to eject. He had to be hospitalized but was able to return to duty only to be made to eject from MiG-21PFL 4223 on 23 April when attacked by the crew of aircraft commander Robert D. Anderson and pilot Fred D. Kjer of the USAF flying a F-4. On 7 November, in the company of Nguyen Hong Nhi, Kinh took off from Phuc Yen to intercept a raid by enemy aircraft, and each pilot claimed an aircraft destroyed, the former a F-105 and the latter a F-4 following which, short of fuel, both had to make emergency landings. With Vu Ngoc Dinh he took off, from Phuc Yen, on 19 November and together they were directed by ground control to an EB-66. Kinh claimed the target was hit by the second

---

[70] One of the claims was A-4C 147799, Navy Attack Squadron (VA)-76, USN, Bon Homme Richard, Lieutenant Charles D. Stackhouse, prisoner of war. One of the claims was possibly A-4E 151116, VA-192, USN, USS Ticonderoga, Lieutenant Commander Francis J. Almberg, recovered. Three VPAF claims were made and shared by Ha Dinh Bon (Ha Bon, Nguyen Bon), Nguyen Ba Dich, Nguyen The Hon, Nguyen Van Bay.

of two R-3S missiles fired and thus made to crash.   Each made a safe landing at Kep and both pilots were given credit for the victory. He was acknowledged to have sent down a F-4 on 19 December while a strike against Hanoi was staged.   Kinh endured an eventful flight on 3 January 1968 after taking off from Kep with Bui Duc Nhu following which each claimed a F-105 destroyed.   When landing, however, he had difficulty and overran the runway following which the canopy of the MiG-21 had to be smashed by a rescue crew to extricate the pilot.   With Dong Van Song, Kinh attacked an EB-66 on 14 January and both were credited with the downing of the aircraft. He was fortunate not to have become a victim of friendly fire when flying with Nguyen Van Lung as escorts to Dang Ngoc Ngu and Nguyen Van Coc on 7 May.   Confusing ground control as well as fire from anti aircraft units and masses of cloud, apparently, flustered the escorted which turned on the escorts, but the error was realized before any firing was done. Having destroyed an AQM-34 on 21 September, a final victory, over what was apparently a F-4 of the USN, was claimed by the Gulf of Tonkin on 26 October. Undertaking further study in the USSR, Kinh assumed Staff positions relating to training and procurement and ultimately rose to the rank of Major General. He was made a Hero Of The Vietnam People's Armed Forces on 28 May 2010. Having flown numerous missions and survived three ejections during combat, Nguyen Dang Kinh eventually retired from military service to assume a position in civil aviation and was to experience the satisfaction of having a son become a pilot in the VPAF.

Known Claims

21/07/1966	AQM-34	921st F.R.	MiG-21
05/12/1966	F-105[71]	921st F.R.	MiG-21
07/11/1967	F-4	921st F.R.	MiG-21PFL 4324
19/11/1967	EB-66[72]	921st F.R.	MiG-21PFL 4324
19/12/1967	F-4	921st F.R.	MiG-21PFL 4326

---

[71] F-105D 62-4331, 421 TFS, 388 TFW, USAF, Major Burriss N. Begley, killed in action.

[72] A single VPAF claim was made and shared by Nguyen Dang Kinh and Vu Ngoc Dinh.

03/01/1968	F-105[73]	921st F.R.	MiG-21PFM 5018
14/01/1968	EB-66[74]	921st F.R.	MiG-21
21/09/1968	AQM-34	921st F.R.	MiG-21
26/10/1968	F-4	921st F.R.	MiG-21

Nguyen Duc Soat

Nguyễn Đức Soát

Official Victories: 6

Nguyen Duc Soat was born on 24 June 1946 in Phu Xuyen District, Hanoi, close to the Red River, and joined the military on 5 July 1965. After being trained in the USSR between 1965 and 1968 to fly the MiG-21, he benefited from instruction given by Nguyen Van Coq and Pham Thanh Ngan and was credited with the destruction of an AQM-34 on 13 March 1969, having become a member of the 921st Fighter Regiment, and participated in the memorial flypast for Ho Chi Minh on 9 September. Soat transferred to the 927th Fighter Regiment in 1972 and claimed an A-7 destroyed on 23 May. On 24 June he took off to intercept a USAF strike on an industrial target at Thai Nguyen in the company of Ngo Duy Thu and claimed a F-4 sent down before returning to Phuc Yen. The pair was again in combat on 27 June and each was credited with a F-4 destroyed by the border between the DRV and the KL; apparently Soat fired two R-3S missiles which both hit the target. He was credited with a victory on 30 July after damaging a F-4 which was abandoned by the crew over the Gulf of Tonkin. An interception on 26 August brought Soat, flying a camouflaged MiG-21, recognition for a claim over a F-4 struck by a missile in the empennage

---

[73] Possibly F-105D 58-1157, 469 TFS, 388 TFW, USAF, Colonel James E. Bean, prisoner of war.

[74] EB-66C 55-0388, 41 TEWS, 355 TFW, USAF, Major Pollard H. Mercer (pilot), recovered, died of wounds 20/1/1968, Major Thomas W. Sumpter, prisoner of war, Major Irby D. Terrell, prisoner of war, Captain Hubert C. Walker, prisoner of war, First Lieutenant Ronald M. Lebert, prisoner of war, First Lieutenant Attilio Pedroli, recovered, First Lieutenant James E. Thompson, recovered. A single VPAF claim was made and shared by Nguyen Dang Kinh and Dong Van Song.

being, it would seem, the only USMC aircraft lost as a result of aerial combat during the American War. He was recognized for sending down a F-4 flying as an escort to a strike on a railway target, on 12 October, despite poor weather conditions. Nguyen Duc Soat was made a Hero Of The Vietnam People's Armed Forces on 11 January 1973, served as Deputy Chief of Staff of the VPA and, attaining the rank of Lieutenant General, was made the Commander of the VPAF and even became a published historian of the service.

Known Claims

13/03/1969	AQM-34	921st F.R.	MiG-21
23/05/1972	A-7[75]	927th F.R.	MiG-21
24/06/1972	F-4[76]	927th F.R.	MiG-21PFM 5020
27/06/1972	F-4[77]	927th F.R.	MiG-21PFM 5057
30/07/1972	F-4[78]	927th F.R.	MiG-21
26/08/1972	F-4[79]	927th F.R.	MiG-21
12/10/1972	F-4[80]	927th F.R.	MiG-21

[75] Possibly A-7B 154405, VF-93, USN, USS Midway, Commander Charles E. Barnett, killed in action.

[76] F-4E 68-0315, 421 TFS, 366 TFW, USAF, Captain David B. Grant (pilot), prisoner of war, Captain William D. Beekman, prisoner of war.

[77] Possibly F-4E 68-0314, 308 TFS, 31 TFW attached to 432 TRW, USAF, Lieutenant Colonel Farrell J. Sullivan (pilot), killed in action, Captain Richard L. Francis, prisoner of war.

[78] F-4D 66-7597, 523 TFS, 405 Fighter Wing (FW) attached to 432 TRW, USAF, Captain G. B. Brooks (pilot), recovered, Captain J. M. McAdams, recovered.

[79] F-4J 155811, Marine Fighter Attack Squadron-232, Marine Aircraft Group-15, USMC, First Lieutenant Sam G. Cordova (pilot), killed or died, date unknown, First Lieutenant Darrell L. Borders, recovered.

[80] F-4E 69-0276, 469 TFS, 388 TFW, USAF, Captain Myron A. Young (pilot), prisoner of war, First Lieutenant Cecil H. Brunson, prisoner of war.

Nguyen Hong Nhi

Nguyễn Hồng Nhị

Official Victories: 8

Born on 22 December 1936 in Hoai Nhon District, Binh Dinh Province, Nguyen Hong Nhi enlisted in the armed forces on 25 May 1952 and, following the enactment of the Geneva Agreements, traveled north to continue the struggle for liberation and reunification from within the DRV. He joined the 910th Air Training Regiment and was taught to pilot helicopters before being chosen to study in the USSR, doing so between 1961 and 1964, so as to be able to fly the MiG-21. Nhi became a member of the 921st Fighter Regiment in 1964 and was the first to claim a victory for the unit flying the MiG-21, doing so, on 4 March 1966 by destroying an AQM-34 at an altitude of 18000 metres (59,055 feet) and was, afterwards, personally decorated by Ho Chi Minh for the deed. Engaged with F-4s while trying to intercept EB-66s when flying with Dong Van Song on 26 April, he was forced to eject and suffered spinal injury; the aircraft being destroyed by the crew of aircraft commander Paul J. Gilmore and pilot William T. Smith. Having recovered, Nhi claimed two reconnaissance aircraft shot down, a RF-4 on 31 August 1967 and a RF-101 on 10 September. When flying with Dong Van Song on 9 October, Nhi claimed a F-105, part of a raid travelling to bomb the railway at Quang Hein, destroyed by a R-3S missile which entered the tailpipe of the target. Taking off from Phuc Yen on 7 November, he was credited with shooting down a F-105 while accompanied by Nguyen Dang Kinh who claimed the destruction of a F-4 following which both ran short of fuel and had to make emergency landings which each pilot completed successfully. Nhi claimed a F-105 destroyed over Thanh Son on 17 December. On 1 August 1968, while flying with Nguyen Dang Kinh and Pham Van Mao, in a MiG-21 with a malfunctioning throttle he engaged F-8s and fired two R-3S missiles at one which was claimed destroyed, but while struggling with another F-8 was set upon by an additional brace. The MiG-21 was struck by two missiles when climbing, the one which destroyed the aircraft being fired by Norman K. McCoy, forcing Nhi to eject and, as a result, not be able to return to the 921st Fighter Regiment until three days later having been held as prisoner for a time as, speaking with the accent of one from the south of the country, local people believed a member of the VNAF had been captured! After the experience of ejection and capture he was given leave and passed time in the Tam Dao District to enjoy the beauty of the Red River delta where Nguyen Thi Tanh Dao, a doctor who had once helped to capture an American pilot, was met; the two would later marry an raise a family together. On 9 September 1969 Nhi had the honour of leading the memorial flight of 12 MiG-21s of the 921st Fighter Regiment flying past over Ba Dinh Square to commemorate the life of Ho Chi Minh. He was made a Hero Of The Vietnam People's Armed Forces on 18 June 1969 and, having been the commander of the 927th Fighter Regiment from 1972 to 1973, would rise to the rank of Major General. Later, Nguyen Hong Nhi would work within the Civil Aviation Administration of Vietnam and, eventually, became the Director of the organization.

Known Claims

04/03/1966	AQM-34	921st F.R.	MiG-21F-13
31/08/1967	RF-4	921st F.R.	MiG-21
10/09/1967	RF-101	921st F.R.	MiG-21
26/09/1967	F-4	921st F.R.	MiG-21
09/10/1967	F-105[81]	921st F.R.	MiG-21F-13 4421
07/11/1967	F-105[82]	921st F.R.	MiG-21PFL 4326
17/12/1967	F-105[83]	921st F.R.	MiG-21
01/08/1968	F-8	921st F.R.	MiG-21

Nguyen Ngoc Do

Nguyễn Ngọc Độ

Official Victories: 6

---

[81] F-105D 60-0434, 34 TFS, 388 TFW, USAF, Major James A. Clements, prisoner of war.

[82] Possibly F-105D 60-0430, 469 TFS, 388 TFW, USAF, Major William C. Diehl, prisoner of war, believed to have died while prisoner of war.

[83] Possibly F-105 60-0422, 469 TFS, 388 TFW, USAF, First Lieutenant Jeffrey T. Ellis, prisoner of war.

Nguyen Ngoc Do was born on 1 November 1934 in Thanh Chuong District, Nghe An Province, joined the military on 16 June 1953, and was trained in the PRC from 1956 to 1964 to, eventually, fly the MiG-17 and thereafter became a member of the 921st Fighter Regiment. Subsequently, in 1966 he was chosen for conversion to the MiG-21 in the DRV. On 2 January 1967 two flights of MiG-21s took off from Phuc Yen only to be attacked by the pilots of the 8th TFW conducting Operation Bolo; Do, in MiG-21PFL 4029, was the one pilot of the second flight of four who was made to eject. On 30 April, as the result of an attack on a formation of F-105s, he and accompanying pilot Nguyen Van Coc each claimed one downed and then had the satisfaction of seeing the ordnance dropped from the other aircraft. Do made a claim for the destruction of a F-105 on 5 May which, apparently, was engaged in AAA suppression. He was flying with Pham Thanh Ngan on 20 July when the pair were credited with a F-4 sent down over Nho Quen and they again operated together on 16 September, flying MiG-21s supplied by the RC, with each pilot claiming a RF-101 despatched. Ignoring escorts to strike at the aircraft carrying the bombs, on 5 February 1968, Do flew over F-4s to attack F-105s and claimed one destroyed with a R-3S missile. Having been made a Hero Of The Vietnam People's Armed Forces on 25 August 1970, he served as the commander of the 921st Fighter Regiment from 1972 until 1974. Nguyen Ngoc Do was to attain the rank of Major General prior to retiring from service in 2000.

Known Claims

30/04/1967	F-105[84]	921st F.R.	MiG-21PFL 4227
05/05/1967	F-105[85]	921st F.R.	MiG-21PFL 4320
20/07/1967	F-4[86]	921st F.R.	MiG-21
02/08/1967	F-105	921st F.R.	MiG-21

---

[84] F-105D 59-1726, 354 TFS, 355 TFW, USAF, First Lieutenant Robert A. Abbott, prisoner of war.

[85] Possibly F-105D 61-0198, 357 TFS, 355 TFW, USAF, First Lieutenant James R. Shively, prisoner of war.

[86] A single VPAF claim was made and shared by Nguyen Ngoc Do and Pham Thanh Ngan.

16/09/1967	RF-101[87]	921st F.R.	MiG-21F-13 4420
27/09/1967	F-105	921st F.R.	MiG-21PFL 4320
05/02/1968	F-105	921st F.R.	MiG-21PFL 4320

Nguyen Nhat Chieu

Nguyễn Nhật Chiêu

Official Victories: 6

Born in 1934, in Nam Sach District, Hai Duong Province, Nguyen Nhat Chieu enlisted in the armed forces on 12 December 1953 and was active in the struggle to liberate Vietnam from French control. When meeting Ho Chi Minh on 25 August 1956 he was asked to become a pilot and so volunteered to travel to the PRC for training which lasted between 1956 and 1964 and thereafter, upon having learned to fly the MiG-17, he was assigned to the 921st Fighter Regiment and on 6 August 1964, the day the VPAF first assumed readiness, sat at Phuc Yen in a MiG-17 as one of the second pair of pilots put on alert status waiting for an enemy intrusion. While having been forced to eject during an engagement with aircraft of the USS Midway on 17 June 1965 following which the wounded pilot travelled some three days through forest before gaining assistance, on 20 September, Chieu became involved in an action over Yen Tu and pursued a F-4 towards the Gulf of Tonkin letting go bursts of fire at ever closer range until running out of ammunition, thus, causing the target to catch fire and crash in the vicinity of Nha Ham. He was one of a group of pilots chosen for conversion training to learn to fly the MiG-21, in the DRV, with the intention of bringing the type to service in January 1966. Revelling in the superior performance of the MiG-21, Chieu claimed a F-4 destroyed on 20 May 1967 and, on 17 July, lead an element of the 921st Fighter Regiment on an attack, well coordinated with ground control, upon F-8s in proximity to Lang Chanh during which Nguyen Van Ly claimed a success. He and Nguyen Van Coc, flew with two flights of four MiG-17s to engage a

---

[87] Either RF-101C 56-0180, 20 TRS, 432 TRW, USAF, Major Bobby R. Bagley, prisoner of war or RF-101C 56-0181, 20 TRS, 432 TRW, USAF, Captain Robert E. Patterson, recovered.

formation of enemy aircraft approaching Hanoi on 23 August and each claimed F-4s destroyed using the R-3S missile, before the former, emerging from a cloud, fired at the latter in error causing damage; being an ironic occasion when MiG-21 cannon was used and the target struck.   Again flying together, after taking off from Phuc Yen, on 7 October both of the pilots claimed F-105s sent down.   In the air with Dang Ngoc Ngu, on 29 October, Chieu was attacked but able to avoid a AAM then fired a R-3S missile which, apparently, set a F-4 alight. Having served as a combat pilot for approximately two years, flying some 600 sorties, claiming victories in a Shenyang J-5 and in the MiG-21, Nguyen Nhat Chieu, was assigned to the 927th Fighter Regiment, made a Hero Of The Vietnam People's Armed Forces on 31 December 1973, and ultimately rose to the rank of Senior Colonel before retiring from service to take up a life on the land by farming.

Known Claims

20/09/1965	F-4	921st F.R.	Shenyang J-5 2217
20/05/1967	F-4	921st F.R.	MiG-21PFL 4227
23/08/1967	2 F-4s[88]	921st F.R.	MiG-21PFL 4228
07/10/1967	F-105[89]	921st F.R.	MiG-21
29/10/1967	F-4	921st F.R.	MiG-21F-13 4426

Nguyen Phi Hung

Nguyễn Phi Hùng

Official Victories: 5

---

[88] Either F-4D 66-0238, 555 TFS, 8 TFW, USAF, Major Charles R. Tyler (pilot), prisoner of war, Captain Ronald N. Sittner, killed or died, date unknown or F-4D 66-0247, 555 TFS, 8 TFW, USAF, Captain Larry E. Carrigan (pilot), prisoner of war, First Lieutenant Charles Lane Jr., killed in action.

[89] Either F-105F 63-8330, 13 TFS, 388 TFW, USAF, Captain Joseph D. Howard (pilot), recovered, Captain George L. Shamblee, recovered or F-105D 60-0444, 34 TFS, 388 TFW, USAF, Major Wayne E. Fullam, killed in action.

Nguyen Phi Hung was born in 1942 and studied in Hanoi but rather than go to college joined the military in May 1961. He was assigned to the 910th Air Training Regiment in 1961 and learned to fly the MiG-17 in the USSR. Having served with the 919th Air Transport Regiment between 1964 and 1965 and, again, with the 910th Air Training Regiment between 1965 and 1966, Hung became a member of the 923rd Fighter Regiment in 1966. Frequently in combat through the latter months of 1967, often flying either MiG-17F 2064 or MiG-17F 2087 and, on occasion, Shenyang J-5 2315, Hung was able to claim four victories. Flying with Nguyen Phu Ninh on 9 July 1968 he was directed by ground control to intercept F-8s and claimed one shot down into the Gulf of Tonkin. Having been ordered to return, the pair were attacked when over Nghia Dan and Hung turned back to engage the F-8s, alone, despite having but a slight amount of both fuel and ammunition left. At least one AAM was avoided but the MiG-17 flown was eventually struck by another and subsequently by cannon shells as well and, too low to eject, he was killed, being the victim of John B. Nichols flying a F-8 of VF-191 of the USS Bon Homme Richard who saw the target disintegrate. Serving at the rank of Senior Lieutenant when killed, Nguyen Phi Hung was posthumously made a Hero of the Vietnam People's Armed Forces on 10 December 1994.

Known Claims

07/10/1967	F-4	923rd F.R.	MiG-17
06/11/1967	F-105[90]	923rd F.R.	MiG-17
19/11/1967	F-4[91]	923rd F.R.	MiG-17
19/12/1967	F-105	923rd F.R.	MiG-17
09/07/1968	F-8	923rd F.R.	MiG-17

[90] Possibly F-105D 62-4286, 469 TFS, 388 TFW, USAF, Major Robert W. Hagerman, killed in action.

[91] F-4B 152304, VF-151, USN, USS Coral Sea, Lieutenant (Junior Grade) James E. Teague (pilot), killed in action, Lieutenant (Junior Grade) Theodore G. Stier, prisoner of war.

Nguyen The Hon

Nguyễn Thế Hôn

Official Victories: 3

Nguyen The Hon was one of a group selected to train to be pilots in the PRC in 1959 who eventually qualified to fly the MiG-17. Returning to the DRV, he joined the 923rd Fighter Regiment and was soon flying in combat. Hon first claimed a victory on 13 July 1966 following a battle with a F-8. On 24 April 1967 he was a member of a flight flying camouflaged MiG-17s flown at minimal height while maintaining radio silence until in proximity of USN aircraft attacking Kep. Suddenly gaining speed and altitude the four pilots attacked and destroyed two F-4s before making off at the lowest level possible. The following day Hon flew as part of a flight that, having flown to Kien An, mounted an operation against a USN strike on targets in the vicinity of Haiphong that resulted in claims for two A-4s shot down. Though pursued by F-8s, one of which Hon engaged and claimed to have destroyed, the four pilots flew along the Red River to land safely at Gia Lam. On 14 May, confronting a USAF strike on the Ha Dong barracks with Le Hai, he engaged F-4s of the 366th TFW. Heard to call out a victory over one on radio, Nguyen The Hon, serving at the rank of Senior Lieutenant, was then attacked by another and killed but would be recognized as a Hero of the Vietnam People's Armed Forces.

Known Claims

13/07/1966	F-8	923rd F.R.	MiG-17
24/04/1967	2 F-4s[92]	923rd F.R.	MiG-17
25/04/1967	2 A-4s,		

---

92 One of the claims was F-4B 153000, VF-114, USN, USS Kitty Hawk, Lieutenant Commander Charles E. Southwick (pilot), recovered, Ensign James W. Laing, recovered. Two VPAF claims were made and shared by Nguyen Ba Dich, Nguyen The Hon, Nguyen Van Bay, Vo Van Man.

	1 F-8[93]	923rd F.R.	MiG-17
14/05/1967	F-4	923rd F.R.	MiG-17

Nguyen Tien Sam
Nguyễn Tiến Sâm
Official Victories: 5

Born on 15 June 1946 in the Thanh Tri District, Hanoi, near the Red River, Nguyen Tien Sam enlisted in the military on 2 June 1965. After graduating from the Hanoi University of Science And Technology he receiving training at the Krasnador Flight Officer's Training School in the USSR. Sam joined the 921st Fighter Regiment and was first in combat on 16 June 1968 and had to eject from a MiG-21 on 9 February 1969 which had run out of fuel. In 1972 he transferred to the 927th Fighter Regiment. Benefiting from precise ground control on 5 July 1972 after taking off from Phuc Yen, while flying over Kep, Sam emerged from cloud positioned directly behind and below enemy aircraft. He fired one AAM, which exploded prematurely, so, with range closing, a second AAM was fired which ran true causing a massive explosion which could not be avoided. Sam flew through the flame and wreckage which caused the engine of the MiG-21 piloted, PFM 5020, to cut out. Fortunately he was able to restart the engine of the aircraft which was made black by the fulmination of the F-4 destroyed and then dove back into cloud to return to Phuc Yen and claim a victory as did accompanying pilot Ha Vinh Thanh. The two pilots, again flying together on 24 July, became involved in combat with F-4s and both attacked with R-3S missiles, those launched by Thanh missed but those fired by Sam struck the target which, though damaged, was able to be flown to the Gulf of Tonkin, there, to be abandoned by the crew. Before the month was out, on 29 July, he was credited with another F-4 destroyed following a

---

[93] One of the claims was A-4C 147799, VA-76, USN, Bon Homme Richard, Lieutenant Charles D. Stackhouse, prisoner of war. One of the claims was possibly A-4E 151116, VA-192, USN, USS Ticonderoga, Lieutenant Commander Francis J. Almberg, recovered. Three VPAF claims were made and shared by Ha Dinh Bon (Ha Bon, Nguyen Bon), Nguyen Ba Dich, Nguyen The Hon, Nguyen Van Bay.

confusing combat in which one USAF aircraft may well have fired on another USAF aircraft. Sam was credited with a victory on 12 September after firing an AAM when flying at a speed approaching Mach 1 that set a F-4 aflame. On 5 October he shot down a F-4 that was pursuing Bui Duc Nhu, however, on 12 October he attracted the attention of several F-4s while Nguyen Duc Soat prepared to attack and flew such evasive manoeuvres as to loose consciousness and control of the MiG-21 flown requiring ejection upon reviving. Made a Hero Of The Vietnam People's Armed Forces on 11 January 1973, Nguyen Tien Sam was subsequently to graduate from the General Staff Academy of the USSR, attain the rank of Senior Colonel and serve as Chief of Staff of the VPAF before becoming the Deputy Minister of Transport in 1998.

Known Claims

05/07/1972	F-4[94]	927th F.R.	MiG-21PFM 5020
24/07/1972	F-4[95]	927th F.R.	MiG-21
29/07/1972	F-4[96]	927th F.R.	MiG-21PFM 5014
12/09/1972	F-4[97]	927th F.R.	MiG-21PFM 5017
05/10/1972	F-4[98]	927th F.R.	MiG-21

---

[94] Either F4E 67-0339, 34 TFS, 388 TFW, Major William J. Elander (pilot), prisoner of war, First Lieutenant Donald K. Logan, prisoner of war or F-4E 67-0296, 34 TFS, 388 TFW, USAF, Captain William A. Spencer (pilot), prisoner of war, First Lieutenant Brian J. Seek, prisoner of war.

[95] Possibly F-4E 66-0369, 421 TFS, 366 TFW, USAF, Captain Samuel A. Hodnett (pilot), recovered, First Lieutenant David M. Fallert, recovered.

[96] F-4E 66-0367, 4 TFS, 366 TFW, USAF, Captain James D. Kula (pilot), prisoner of war, Captain Melvin K. Matsui, prisoner of war.

[97] F-4E 69-7266, 336 TFS, 4 TFW, attached to 8 TFW, USAF, Captain Rudolph V. Zuberbuhler (pilot), prisoner of war, Captain Frederick C. McMurray, prisoner of war.

[98] F-4D 66-8738, 335 TFS, 4 TFW attached to 8 TFW, USAF, Captain Keith H. Lewis (pilot), prisoner of war, Captain John H. Alpers, prisoner of war.

Nguyen Van Bay
Nguyễn Văn Bảy
Official Victories: 7

Nguyen Van Bay was born on 2 February 1936 in Sa Dec Province, in the Mekong Delta, being one of 11 children, originally with the name Nguyen Van Hoa. He avoided an arranged marriage thereafter joining the armed forces on 3 April 1954. Taking on the name Nguyen Van Bay, the decision was made to stay north of the 17th parallel following the signing of the Geneva Accords. He became a member of the 910th Air Training Regiment and was sent to the PRC for flight training in 1960. While in training Bay flew the CJ-6, variants of the MiG-15 and, the aircraft with which fame would be found, the MiG-17, struggling with air sickness and eventually amassing some 200 hours of flight time about 100 of which were in the latter type. Though, from 1964, a member of the 921st Fighter Regiment, he joined the 923rd Fighter Regiment in 1965, first flying in combat as a member of the unit on 6 October 1965, apparently in action against an element of VF-151 of the USS Coral Sea, and making a forced landing at Noi Bai after an AIM-7 missile exploded in close proximity tearing some 82 holes in the MiG-17 flown. On 26 April, having been married to Tran The Nien days before, between periods on alert, in a ceremony that lasted 15 minutes, Bay claimed a victory over a F-4 and on 29 April claimed a F-105 shot down. He was part of an element which was given credit for downing a RF-8 and a F-8 on 21 June 1966 then on 29 June further success was acknowledged when flying as one of a flight which was credited with the destruction of two F-105s over Tam Dao. Flying from Gia Lam and being directed by Le Thanh Chon, who had experience flying the MiG-17, Bay flew with Vo Van Man on 5 September to intercept a strike. Carefully guided by ground control, he was able to attack a F-8 from behind and, after the target had been struck by cannon shells, saw the pilot, Wilfred K. Abbott, eject to become a prisoner of war. Success came on 16 September when Bay closed on a F-4, participating in an attack on the Dap Cau bridge, to less than 150 metres (492 feet) fired, corrected, fired and then looked back to see the target burning. A difficult combat at low level on 21 September resulted in a narrow escape from F-4s which flew away just when he made the decision to eject thus allowing for a landing when all but out of fuel.

Having been made a Hero Of The Vietnam People's Armed Forces on 1 January 1967, Bay was often invited to dine with Ho Chi Minh but he continued to fly in combat, claiming a F-4 destroyed for a fifth confirmed, individual, victory, thus, becoming the first Vietnamese pilot to be officially recognized as an ace. He participated in an action on 24 April 1967 with fellow members of the 923rd Fighter Regiment employing new tactics developed to surprise the pilots of enemy aircraft. After taking off from Gia Lam, Bay, flying in a flight of camouflaged aircraft at low level, was directed by ground control toward a force sent to attack Kep and Hoa Lac. Gaining speed and climbing, the pilots of the MiG-17s appeared behind F-4s from VF-114 of USS Kitty Hawk and opened fire, then dove for cover to claim two despatched. Flying from Kien An on 25 April, Bay was a member of a flight given credit for downing three aircraft, two A-4s and a F-8. On a sortie on 29 April in the vicinity of Ba Vi he outmaneuvered F-4s and was able to gain what would be a final victory. It was decided that Bay would best serve the DRV by fulfilling administrative tasks rather than risking life. He flew a final mission on 1 May, May Day, and, having survived more than 500 sorties, many at the controls of MiG-17 2505, was then excluded from combat operations and designated a Command Duty Officer and would be made the leader of the memorial flight of 12 MiG-17s of the 923rd Fighter Regiment which flew over the service to memorialize Ho Chi Minh on 9 September 1969. Later decorated by the RC, Nguyen Van Bay remained in the VPAF until 1991, rising to the rank of Senior Colonel, then, with feet on the ground and in the water, took up the life of a farmer, growing fruit and raising fish. He gave interviews to those interested in the VPAF and often met with pilots of the American air forces even travelling to the USA in 2017, with other Vietnamese airmen, to participate in a conference entitled From Dogfights To Detente. Nguyen Van Bay died, after suffering a brain haemorrhage, in the evening of 22 September 2019 in Ho Chi Minh City.

Known Claims

| 26/04/1966 | F-4 | 923rd F.R. | MiG-17F 2019 |
| 29/04/1966 | F-105[99] | 923rd F.R. | MiG-17 |

---

[99] Possibly F-105D 62-4304, 333 TFS, 355 TFW, USAF, First Lieutenant Donald W. Bruch, killed in action.

21/06/1966	1 RF-8,		
	1 F-8[100]	923rd F.R.	MiG-17
29/06/1966	2 F-105s[101]	923rd F.R.	MiG-17
05/09/1966	F-8[102]	923rd F.R.	MiG-17
16/09/1966	F-4[103]	923rd F.R.	MiG-17
21/01/1967	F-105[104]	923rd F.R.	MiG-17
24/04/1967	2 F-4s[105]	923rd F.R.	MiG-17F 2537
25/04/1967	2 A-4s,		
	1 F-8[106]	923rd F.R.	MiG-17

---

[100] One of the claims was possibly RF-8A 146830, Detachment L, VFP-63, USN, USS Hancock, Lieutenant Leonard C. Eastman, prisoner of war. One of the claims was F-8E 149152, VF-211, USN, USS Hancock, Lieutenant Commander Cole Black, prisoner of war. Two VPAF claims were made and shared by Duong Trung Tan, Nguyen Van Bay, Pham Thanh Chung, Phan Van Tuc.

[101] One of the claims was possibly F-105D 60-0460, 333 TFS, 355 TFW, USAF, Captain Murphy N. Jones, prisoner of war. Two VPAF claims were made and shared by Nguyen Van Bay, Phan Van Tuc, Tran Huyen, Vo Van Man.

[102] F-8E 150896, VF111, USN, USS Oriskany, Captain Wilfred K. Abbott (USAF pilot on exchange), prisoner of war.

[103] F-4C 63-7643, 555 TFS, 8 TFW, USAF, Major John L. Robertson (pilot), killed in action, First Lieutenant Hubert E. Buchanan, prisoner of war.

[104] F-105D 58-1156, 421 TFS, 388 TFW, USAF, Captain W. R. Wyatt, recovered.

[105] One of the claims was F-4B 153000, VF-114, USN, USS Kitty Hawk, Lieutenant Commander Charles E. Southwick (pilot), recovered, Ensign James W. Laing, recovered. Two VPAF claims were made and shared by Nguyen Ba Dich, Nguyen The Hon, Nguyen Van Bay, Vo Van Man.

[106] One of the claims was A-4C 147799, VA-76, USN, Bon Homme Richard, Lieutenant Charles D. Stackhouse, prisoner of war. One of the claims was possibly A-4E 151116, VA-192, USN, USS Ticonderoga, Lieutenant Commander Francis J. Almberg, recovered. Three VPAF claims were made and shared by Ha Dinh Bon (Ha Bon, Nguyen Bon), Nguyen Ba Dich, Nguyen The Hon, Nguyen Van Bay.

29/04/1967   F-4[107]   923rd F.R.   MiG-17

Nguyen Van Coc

Nguyễn Văn Cốc

Official Victories: 9

Born on 15 December 1942 in Viet Yen District, Bac Giang Province, Nguyen Van Coc was the son of a Viet Minh cadre killed in 1947 during the struggle against the French having been thrown down a well for not revealing the location Viet Minh shelters. The family moved from the area to the vicinity of an airfield where he became fascinated by aviation. A member of the VPAF from 1961, after beginning training, Coc was selected to travel to the USSR to hone flying skills and there learned to fly the MiG-17 between 1962 and 1964. He returned to the DRV to serve with the 921st Fighter Regiment only to be selected to train to fly the MiG-21 and was, therefore, sent to the USSR in 1965. Back to service in the DRV in June 1966 to train others, Coc took to the air on operations in 1966 and, on 14 December claimed a victory when flying with Dong Van De; in fact De was credited with two F-105s shot down but Coc was denied confirmation of the F-105 believed to have been despatched. Airborne on 2 January 1967, when two flights of four MiG-21s of the 921st Fighter Regiment were beset by F-4s of the USAF undertaking Operation Bolo, flying in the second of the two, he was fortunate not to be forced to eject as several comrades were. On 30 April Coc was flying with Nguyen Ngoc Do when F-105s were encountered at a lower altitude and the two dove to the attack; each was able to destroy one and cause the remainder to drop the ordnance carried. Airborne in the company of Pham Thanh Ngan on 4 May, an attempt to attack F-105s drew the attention of escorts. After being pursued at length by a F-4 flown by aircraft commander Robin Olds and pilot William D. Lafever from which four missiles were fired, he was, eventually, forced to eject from MiG-21PFL 4325 which had been damaged by an explosion behind the

---

[107] Possibly F-4C 64-0670, 389 TFS, 366 TFW, USAF, First Lieutenant Loren H. Torkleson (pilot), prisoner of war, First Lieutenant George J. Pollin, killed in action.

tailpipe at an altitude of 100 metres (328 feet) some 500 metres (1,640 feet) from the runway at Phuc Yen. Coc was lucky to survive the perplexing interception of an attack on the Yen Vien rail yard on 23 August. After claiming a F-4 struck by a R-3S missile and sent down, he flew through cannon fire from Nguyen Nhat Chieu which caused significant damage and, despite having requested to continue the mission, he was ordered to return to base immediately where the MiG-21 flown was found to have ingested pieces of the F-4 that had been destroyed, some of which were found in the intake centre body. Coc claimed the destruction of a F-105 on 7 October and additional F-105s on 18 November, when four of 16 attackers of the 388 TFS were lost during a strike on Phuc Yen, and, despite poor weather conditions, on 20 November to then be recognized as an ace. Flying with Nguyen Van Ly on 12 December, he was credited with a victory over a F-105 having rolled over the target to look down and see the aircraft which had been hit by the R-3S missile fired in flames. On 3 February 1968 Coc and Pham Thanh Ngan, flying a fourth sortie of the day together, attacked a pair of F-102s with each firing an AAM; that fired by the former missed while that fired by the latter destroyed the target. On 7 May, despite the frustration of having been shot at by Vietnamese AAA and directed to attack Vietnamese aircraft, he pursued a F-4 from Do Luong towards the coast, eventually firing a R-3S missile which struck the and destroyed the target. He was made a Hero Of The Vietnam People's Armed Forces on 18 June 1969 and was fortunate to be able to meet the gravely ill Ho Chi Minh, and be publicly praised by Uncle Ho. He was subsequently credited with the destruction of three AQM-34s, the last being shot down in collaboration with Pham Thanh Nam on 3 August 1969, and to be recognized as the leading ace of the VPAF with nine confirmed victories. Having flown some 550 sorties, Nguyen Van Coc was removed from combat operations to instruct pilots and would be selected for cosmonaut training before ultimately being rejected for reasons of health, but served as the Commander of the VPAF between 1996 and 1997 and would remain in the service until 2002 attaining the rank of Lieutenant General and taking the role of Chief Inspector of the Ministry Of National Defence though in retirement was to suffer from a debilitating illness.

Known Claims

14/12/1966	F-105	921st F.R.	MiG-21
30/04/1967	F-105[108]	921st F.R.	MiG-21PFL 4325
23/08/1967	F-4[109]	921st F.R.	MiG-21PFL 4227
07/10/1967	F-105[110]	921st F.R.	MiG-21
18/11/1967	F-105[111]	921st F.R.	MiG-21PFL 4326
20/11/1967	F-105[112]	921st F.R.	MiG-21
12/12/1967	F-105	921st F.R.	MiG-21
07/05/1968	F-4[113]	921st F.R.	MiG-21PFL 4326
04/06/1968	AQM-34	921st F.R.	MiG-21
08/11/1968	AQM-34	921st F.R.	MiG-21
03/08/1969	AQM-34[114]	921st F.R.	MiG-21

---

[108] F-105F 62-4447, 357 TFS, 355 TFW, USAF, Major Leo K. Thorsness (pilot), prisoner of war, Captain Harold E. Johnson, prisoner of war.

[109] Either F-4D 66-0238, 555 TFS, 8 TFW, USAF, Major Charles R. Tyler (pilot), prisoner of war, Captain Ronald N. Sittner, killed or died, date unknown or F-4D 66-0247, 555 TFS, 8 TFW, USAF, Captain Larry E. Carrigan (pilot), prisoner of war, First Lieutenant Charles Lane Jr., killed in action.

[110] Either F-105F 63-8330, 13 TFS, 388 TFW, USAF, Captain Joseph D. Howard (pilot), recovered, Captain George L. Shamblee, recovered or F-105D 60-0444, 34 TFS, 388 TFW, USAF, Major Wayne E. Fullam, killed in action.

[111] F-105D 60-0497, 469 TFS, 388 TFW, USAF, Lieutenant Colonel William N. Reed, recovered.

[112] Possibly F-105D 61-0124, 469 TFS, 388 TFW, USAF, Captain William W. Butler, prisoner of war.

[113] F-4B 151485, VF-92, USN, USS Enterprise, Lieutenant Commander Ejnar S. Christensen (pilot), recovered, Lieutenant (Junior Grade) Worth A. Kramer, recovered.

[114] One VPAF claim was made and shared by Nguyen Van Coc and Pham Thanh Nam.

Nguyen Van Nghia

Nguyễn Văn Nghĩa

Official Victories: 5

Nguyen Van Nghia was born on 3 May 1946 in Mo Duc District, Quang Ngai Province, but moved to the DRV following the signing of the Geneva Agreements and enlisted in the armed forces in 1963 then became a member of the VPAF in 1965. Following training in the USSR between 1965 and 1968 he was assigned to the 921st Fighter Regiment, often flying MiG-21MF 5114, until becoming a member of the 927th Fighter Regiment in 1972, with which MiG-21PFM 5040 was regularly piloted, to first fly in combat on 6 March. In the air with Nguyen Van Toan, Nghia claimed a F-4 destroyed on both 23 and 24 June. On 6 October, having flown from Phuc Yen with Tran Van Nam, he led an attack on four F-4s and fired a R-3S missile which did not detonate so fired another which caused a fuel cell rupture in the aircraft struck though the crew of pilot J.P. White and WSO A.G. Egge were able to remain in the aircraft until approaching the border of the KL and the KT to be rescued after ejecting.   Following an unsuccessful interception on 8 October Nghia was pursued by four F-4s and managed to avoid AAMs and cannon shells by flying at low altitude at a speed greater than Mach 1 and thereby reach Phuc Yen and safety. He was credited with the destruction of an AQM-34 when flying with Le Van Lap on 24 November and of a F-4 when flying with Le Van Kien on 23 December following which, with the MiG-21 flown all but out of fuel, the instruction to eject was disregarded and an emergency landing was undertaken safely. Made a Hero Of The Vietnam People's Armed Forces on 3 September 1973, Nguyen Van Nghia became the first to fly the F-5 in VPAF service and was ultimately to rise to the rank of Senior Colonel before leaving the military to take a position in civil aviation working with Vietnam Airlines.

Known Claims

| 23/06/1972 | F-4 | 927th F.R. | MiG-21 |

24/06/1972	F-4[115]	927th F.R.	MiG-21PFM 5052
06/10/1972	F-4[116]	927th F.R.	MiG-21
08/10/1972	F-4	927th F.R.	MiG-21
24/11/1972	AQM-34	927th F.R.	MiG-21PFM 5073
23/12/1972	F-4	927th F.R.	MiG-21

Pham Phu Thai

Phạm Phú Thái

Official Victories: 4

Born on 30 December 1949 in Ha Hoa District, Phu Tho Province, joining the armed forces on 5 July 1965 and having been trained at Krasnador Flight Officer's School in the USSR, Pham Phu Thai arrived in Vietnam in February 1968 to continue training for a period of time prior to joining the 921st Fighter Regiment on combat operations. As a result of poor ground control he was shot down while flying a sortie on 10 July, when engaged with F-4s of VF-33, by pilot Roy Cash and RIO Joseph E. Kain; the AIM-9 missile fired breaking off the entire tail section of the MiG-21 flown, but, a successful ejection was made. Remaining on operations, Thai, who was known to fly both MiG-21MF 5138 and 5147, continued to acquire experience and was chosen to participate in the memorial flight for Ho Chi Minh on 9 September 1969, before claiming a F-4 destroyed on 1 June 1972 after having fired two missiles at two targets to begin a period of success. Further victories were claimed over F-4s during the month, one in cooperation with Bui Thanh Liem on the 10th and others on the 13th and the 24th. Again flying together, he and Bui Thanh Liem took off from Yen Bai to intercept F-4s flying in support of a SAR operation when both pilots, from behind the cover of clouds, fired off R-3S missiles following which each of them was credited with the destruction of an enemy aircraft. Thai

---

[115] F-4D 66-7636, 25 TFS, 8 TFW, USAF, First Lieutenant James L. McCarty (pilot), killed in action, First Lieutenant Charles A. Jackson, prisoner of war.

[116] F-4E 69-7573, 307 TFS, 31 TFW attached to 432 TRW, USAF, Captain J. P. White (pilot), recovered, Captain A. G. Egge, recovered.

was forced to eject on 15 October from MiG-21MF 5138 as a result of combat with F-4s. Surviving the conflict, he served in many Staff positions and attained the rank of Lieutenant General. Pham Phu Thai was made a Hero Of The Vietnam People's Armed Forces on 28 May 2010.

Known Claims			
01/06/1972	F-4[117]	921st F.R.	MiG-21PFM 5072
10/06/1972	F-4[118]	921st F.R.	MiG-21
13/06/1972	F-4[119]	921st F.R.	MiG-21
24/06/1972	F-4	921st F.R.	MiG-21
27/06/1972	F-4[120]	921st F.R.	MiG-21PFM 5023

Pham Thanh Ngan

Phạm Thanh Ngân

Official Victories: 8

Pham Thanh Ngan was born on 18 April 1939 in Phu Binh District, Thai Nguyen Province, joined the military on 21 March 1959, and served with the 351st Artillery Division before becoming a member of the VPAF. Sent to the USSR for pilot training in 1961, he returned to the DRV in October 1964 to fly the MiG-17 with the 921st Fighter Regiment. Following further training in the USSR between 1965 and 1966 Ngan became a MiG-21 pilot and often flew MiG-21F-13 4520. He cooperated with Hoang Bieu to

[117] F-4E, 69-7299, 308 TFS, 31 TFW attached to 432 TRW, USAF, Captain G. W. Hawks (pilot), recovered, Captain David B. Dingee, recovered.

[118] A single VPAF claim was made and shared by Bui Thanh Liem and Pham Phu Thai.

[119] F-4E, 67-0365, 308 TFS, 31 TFW attached to 432 TRW, USAF, First Lieutenant Gregg O. Hanson (pilot), prisoner of war, First Lieutenant Richard J. Fulton, prisoner of war.

[120] Either F-4E 69-7271, 4 TFS, 366 TFW, USAF, Captain Lynn A. Aikman (pilot), recovered, Captain Thomas J. Hanton, prisoner of war or F4E 69-7296, 390 TFS, 366 TFW, USAF, Major R. C. Miller (pilot), recovered, First Lieutenant Richard H. McDow, prisoner of war.

destroy an AQM-34 on 14 December and with Nguyen Ngoc Do to down a F-4 on 20 July 1967. The two were again flying together on 16 September, in MiG-21s sent, via the USSR, from the RC, when each shot down a RF-101 over Son La. Ngan was credited with the destruction of two F-4s within a week, one on 3 October that was flown on to the KL before being abandoned by the crew and the other on 7 October that was, apparently, destroyed outright by the R-3S missile fired. Following an inconclusive combat with F-105s and F-4s on 16 November he was left with little fuel as was true for Nguyen Van Ly, so, both pilots were directed to make an emergency landing at the Ningming airbase in the PRC then returned to the DRV the following day. Ngan was flying with Nguyen Van Coc on 18 November when, despite bad weather, each claimed a F-105 shot down, a feat which was repeated by the pilots two days later. The two often flew together and on 3 February 1968, while being directed on a search for an EB-66, they came across two F-102s and attacked, both launching missiles with that fired by Coc missing while that fired by Ngan ran true to destroy the target. Fortunate in not having to eject when the MiG-21 flown was damaged by SAM fired from the USS Long Beach on 22 September, he was given a watch by Ho Chi Minh in December in recognition of services to the DRV, and was made a Hero Of The Vietnam People's Armed Forces on 18 June 1969. Going to study at the Gagarin Air Force Academy in the USSR in September 1970 and returning to the DRV in September 1975, Pham Thanh Ngan, following further study in the USSR at the Vorishilov General Staff Academy, assumed command of the VPAF in April 1989 with the rank of Lieutenant General and later served as a member of the Politburo for a time before retiring from public service in 2002.

Known Claims

14/12/1966	AQM-34[121]	921st F.R.	MiG-21
04/05/1967	F-105	921st F.R.	MiG-21PFL 4324
20/07/1967	F-4[122]	921st F.R.	MiG-21PFL 4324

[121] A single VPAF claim was made and shared by Hoang Bieu and Pham Than Ngan.

[122] A single VPAF claim was made and shared by Nguyen Ngoc Do and Pham Thanh Ngan.

16/09/1967	RF-101[123]	921st F.R.	MiG-21F-13 4520
03/10/1967	F-4[124]	921st F.R.	MiG-21
07/10/1967	F-4[125]	921st F.R.	MiG-21
18/11/1967	F-105[126]	921st F.R.	MiG-21PFL 4324
03/02/1968	F-102[127]	921st F.R.	MiG-21PFM 5030

Phan Van Tuc

Phan Văn Túc

Official Victories: 4

Born in 1934, Phan Van Tuc joined the armed forces in June 1953 and, following the completion of training in the PRC in 1964, began flying the MiG-17 with the 921st Fighter Regiment. He was noted as a pilot of limited ability but having absolute discipline and, thus, often flew off the wing of a leader. When the 921st Fighter Regiment initiated the combat debut of the VPAF over the Song Ma river on 3 April 1965 Tuc was able to claim a victory over an F-8. Having transferred to the 923rd Fighter Regiment, he was flying with an element of the unit on 21 June 1966 when USN aircraft were engaged and a RF-8 and a F-8 were claimed destroyed above Kep; the victories being shared among the four airmen who participated in the attacks. Two claims over F-105s intercepted on the way to Duc Giang were made by four pilots of the unit, including Tuc, on 29 June and each was

---

[123] Either RF-101C 56-0180, 20 TRS, 432 TRW, USAF, Major Bobby R. Bagley, prisoner of war or RF-101C 56-0181, 20 TRS, 432 TRW, USAF, Captain Robert E. Patterson, recovered.

[124] F-4D 66-7564, 435 TFS, 8 TFW, USAF, Major Joseph D. Moore (pilot), recovered, First Lieutenant Stephen B. Gulbrandson, recovered.

[125] Possibly F-4D 65-0727, 555 TFS, 8 TFW, USAF, Major Ivan D. Appleby (pilot), killed in action, Captain William R. Austin, prisoner of war.

[126] F-105F 63-8295, 34 TFS, 388 TFW, USAF, Major Oscar M. Dardeau (pilot), killed in action, Captain Edward W. Lehnhoff, killed in action.

[127] F-102A 56-1166, 509 Fighter Interceptor Squadron, 405 FW, USAF, First Lieutenant Wallace L. Wiggins, killed in action.

acknowledged as a victor. With Nguyen Ba Dich he shared credit for the destruction of a F-105 interfering with SAM operations on 19 April 1967. Phan Van Tuc died in the course of a training flight over Vinh Phuc on 31 December, serving at the rank of Captain, and would, posthumously, be made a Hero Of The Vietnam People's Armed Forces on 28 April 2000.

Known Claims			
03/04/1965	F-8	921st F.R.	MiG-17
21/06/1966	1 RF-8,		
	1 F-8[128]	923rd F.R.	MiG-17F 2077
29/06/1966	2 F-105s[129]	923rd F.R.	MiG-17
19/04/1967	F-105[130]	923rd F.R.	MiG-17

Vo Van Man
Võ Văn Mẫn
Official Victories: 5

Vo Van Man was born in 1939 and enlisted in the military in February 1959 undergoing training to fly the MiG-17 in the PRC between 1960 and 1964, thereafter being assigned to the 921st Fighter Regiment. He joined the 923rd Fighter Regiment in 1965 and participated in a combat on 29 June 1966 when a flight of the unit claimed the destruction of two F-4s. On 19

---

[128] One of the claims was possibly RF-8A 146830, Detachment L, VFP-63, USN, USS Hancock, Lieutenant Leonard C. Eastman, prisoner of war. One of the claims was F-8E 149152, VF-211, USN, USS Hancock, Lieutenant Commander Cole Black, prisoner of war. Two VPAF claims were made and shared by Duong Truong Tan, Nguyen Van Bay, Pham Thanh Chung, Phan Van Tuc.

[129] One of the claims was possibly F-105D 60-0460, 333 TFS, 355 TFW, USAF, Captain Murphy N. Jones, prisoner of war. Two VPAF claims were made and shared by Nguyen Van Bay, Phan Van Tuc, Tran Huyen, Vo Van Man.

[130] F-105F 63-8341, 357 TFS, 355 TFW, USAF, Major Thomas M. Madison (pilot), prisoner of war, Major Thomas J. Sterling, prisoner of war.

July, during an action that had lasted more than 15 minutes, Man flew behind a F-105 attempting to shoot the MiG-17 flown by Nguyen Bien down and hit the target with bursts of cannon fire, thus, gaining a victory, but, was in turn pursued by another F-105 which was only deterred by AAA and an attack by Nguyen Bien over Phuc Yen. Along with Tran Huyen, on 29 July 1966, he was given credit for shooting down a Douglas RC-47 which had been engaged on a classified operation under the code name Project Dogpatch just over the border between the Lao province of Sam Neua and the Vietnamese province of Hoa Binh and on 5 September Nguyen Van Bay and Man were able to surprise the pilots of two F-8s of VF-111 of the USN when emerging from a cloud and each claimed one of the enemy destroyed. Flying in an element of the 923rd Fighter Regiment that managed to induce some 32 F-105s to abandon the ordinance carried on 21 September, Man become involved in a battle with F-4s during which one was so damaged by cannon fire that the crew ultimately had to eject after gaining the Gulf of Tonkin but the MiG-17 piloted sustained damage necessitating a carefully managed landing. He was one of a flight that had taken off from Kien An, where it was possible to shelter aircraft at the base of a mountain, credited with the downing of two F-4s on 24 April 1967. Attempting to attack F-105s on 14 May, Man was engaged by F-4s and claimed one set afire. Moments later he was killed when a AAM fired from a F-4 flown by aircraft commander Samuel O. Bakke and pilot Robert W. Lambert struck J-5 1033 being flown. Vo Van Man had been serving at the rank of Senior Lieutenant and would be made a Hero Of The Vietnam People's Armed Forces, posthumously, on 28 April 2000.

Known Claims

| 29/06/1966 | 2 F-105s[131] | 923rd F.R. | MiG-17 |
| 19/07/1966 | F-105[132] | 923rd F.R. | MiG-17 |

---

[131] One of the claims was possibly F-105D 60-0460, 333 TFS, 355 TFW, USAF, Captain Murphy N. Jones, prisoner of war. Two VPAF claims were made and shared by Nguyen Van Bay, Phan Van Tuc, Tran Huyen, Vo Van Man.

[132] F-105D 59-1755, 354 TFS, 355 TFW, USAF, First Lieutenant Stephen W. Diamond, killed in action.

29/07/1966	RC-47[133]	923rd F.R.	MiG-17F 2047
05/09/1966	F-8	923rd F.R.	MiG-17
21/09/1966	F-4[134]	923rd F.R.	MiG-17
24/04/1967	2 F-4s[135]	923rd F.R.	MiG-17
14/05/1967	F-4	923rd F.R.	Shenyang J-5 1033

Vu Ngoc Dinh

Vũ Ngọc Đỉnh

Official Victories: 6

Born on 12 February 1941, Vu Ngoc Dinh joined the military on 28 March 1959. He trained to fly the MiG-17 in the USSR between 1962 and 1964 then served with the 921st Fighter Regiment before returning to the USSR between 1965 and 1966 to be trained to fly the MiG-21. Back in the DRV with the 921st Fighter Regiment, Dinh claimed to have struck a F-105 with a R-3S missile, when flying with Dong Van Song, on 11 July which subsequently ran out of fuel and crashed in the KL. Further success came later in the year and he was credited with the destruction of a F-105 on 5 December and on 19 December. Dinh was forced to eject, from MiG-21PFL 4222, on 2 January 1967, shortly after taking off from Phuc Yen as were the other members of the flight, Bui Duc Nhu, Nguyen Dang Kinh, Nguyen Duc

---

[133] RC-47D 43-48388, 606 Air Commando Squadron (ACS), 634 Combat Support Group (CSG), USAF, Captain Robert E. Hoskinson (pilot), missing in action, Major Galileo F. Bossio, missing in action, First Lieutenant Vincent A. Chiarello, killed or died, date unknown, Captain Bernard Conklin, killed or died, date unknown, First Lieutenant Robert J. Di Tommaso, missing in action, Staff Sergeant James S. Hall, killed or died, date unknown, Technical Sergeant John M. Mamiya, killed or died, date unknown, Technical Sergeant Herbert E. Smith, killed or died, date unknown. A single VPAF claim was made and shared by Tran Huyen and Vo Van Man.

[134] F-4C 63-7462, 433 TFS, 8 TFW, USAF, Captain Richard G. Kellems (pilot), recovered, First Lieutenant John W. Thomas, recovered.

[135] One of the claims was F-4B 153000, VF-114, USN, USS Kitty Hawk, Lieutenant Commander Charles E. Southwick (pilot), recovered, Ensign James W. Laing, recovered. Two VPAF claims were made and shared by Nguyen Ba Dich, Nguyen The Hon, Nguyen Van Bay, Vo Van Man.

Thuan and Nguyen Ngoc Do of a following flight when five of eight MiG-21s launched were destroyed by USAF F-4s conducting Operation Bolo. He did claim a F-105 on 30 April; a day when members of the 921st Fighter Regiment shot down three and damaged one of the type. Caught from behind by a flight of F-4s on 20 May, ejection was necessary for Dinh after two AAMs exploded in proximity to the MiG-21PFL 4321 flown, damaging the hydraulic system. On 17 December, supported by Nguyen Dang Kinh, he claimed two F-105s shot down over the Red River west of Hanoi. Together with Bui Duc Nhu, on 26 June, Dinh was directed towards F-8s but a AAM fired by Lowell R. Myers of VF-51 flying from USS Bon Homme Richard broke off the stabilizer and fins of the MiG-21 piloted necessitating ejection. He was able to claim a victory following Rolling Thunder and before Linebacker when intercepting a SAR mission mounted in an effort to recover the crew of a F-105 shot down by AAA on 28 January 1970. Flying through the SAR formation Dinh fired an R-3S missile which destroyed a HH-53. He was made a Hero of the Vietnam People's Armed Forces on 25 October 1975. Ultimately attaining the rank of Senior Colonel, Vu Ngoc Dinh later assumed the position of Director of the regional airline Vietnam Air Services.

Known Claims

11/07/1966	F-105[136]	921st F.R.	MiG-21
05/12/1966	F-105	921st F.R.	MiG-21
19/12/1966	F-105	921st F.R.	MiG-21
30/04/1967	F-105[137]	921st F.R.	MiG-21
19/11/1967	EB-66[138]	921st F.R	MiG-21

---

[136] F-105D 61-0121, 355 TFW, 34 TFS, USAF, Major William L. McClelland, recovered. A single VPAF claim was made and shared by Dong Van Song and Vu Ngoc Dinh.

[137] Either F-105D 61-0130, 333 TFS, 355 TFW, USAF, Captain Joseph S. Abbott, prisoner of war or F-105 airframe number undetermined, damaged, Major Albert J. Lenski, 333 TFS, 355 TFW, USAF.

[138] A single VPAF claim was made and shared by Nguyen Dang Kinh and Vu Ngoc Dinh.

| 17/12/1967 | F-105s[139] | 921st F.R. | MiG-21 |
| 28/01/1970 | HH-53[140] | 921st F.R. | MiG-21 |

---

[139] Possibly F-105D, 60-0422, 469 TFS, 388 TFW, USAF, First Lieutenant Jeffrey T. Ellis, prisoner of war.

[140] HH-53, 66-14434, 40 ARRS, USAF, Major Holly G. Bell (pilot), killed in action, Captain Leonard C. Leeser, killed in action, Senior Master Sergeant William D. Pruett, killed in action, Technical Sergeant William C. Sutton, killed in action, Sergeant William C. Shinn, killed in action, Sergeant Gregory L. Anderson, killed in action.

<u>Reunification</u>

Lam Van Lich had endured years of conflict. Born in 1932 in Dinh Thanh Commune of the Gia Rai District, Bac Lieu Province in the Mekong Delta, he fought to end the domination of the French in Vietnam. Following the signing of the Geneva Agreements in 1954, Lich chose to continue the struggle for liberation and reunification in the DRV rather than the RVN and so moved from south to north and as a result had to part from the cherished family. Study to become a pilot in the PRC began in 1956 and would continue until 1964 when the flight back to the DRV was made in a MiG-17 as a member of the 921st Fighter Regiment.

Landing at Phuc Yen on 6 August, Lich was, along with Pham Ngoc Lan, one of the first pilots placed on standby to respond to an aerial attack. He was credited with a victory, over a F-4, following combat with aircraft from the USS Midway on 17 June 1965. Trained to fly the MiG-17PF in the darkness, on 3 February 1966 Lich engaged enemy aircraft in the night and was credited with two A-1s destroyed following which the pilot was invited to meet Ho Chi Minh. Having been made Hero of the Vietnam People's Armed Forces on 1 January 1967, he assumed various positions of command with the 923rd Fighter Regiment and administered the further training of qualified pilots to enhance combat skills. Throughout the conflict Lich was not able to learn of the family left living in the RVN as communication between individuals in the north and in the south was not possible. As with many who left the south to continue the struggle from the north, only with the end of the conflict in 1975 did he have a chance to learn the fate of family members.

When I returned to the south in 1975 I found that many of my own family members had been killed. The pain of those deaths was greater than the sadness I felt for participating in the killing. I was away from home for twenty nine years. I gave my family a few days advance notice that I was coming, but when I entered the house I saw my older sister and mistook her for my mother and when my mother came in she did not recognize me. Even after I introduced myself she kept saying, "Lich?, Lich?" She did not believe it. She insisted on examining my head. When she finally found a familiar mole, she cried out "It is you!"

Even though we were fully prepared for the reunion, we cried our hearts out. During the war my mother was arrested many times. All of her sons were engaged in revolutionary activities so the local government frequently took her in for questioning. For the protection of the family she did not tell the younger members of the family about me ... [many] did not even know I existed.[141]

In spite of the best efforts of many, with remarkable resolve, and at a tremendous cost, reunification had been achieved by the women, children and men of the nation for families of Vietnamese and for the people of Vietnam.

---

[141] Lam Van Lich quoted in Appy, Christian G., ed., Patriots The Vietnam War Remembered From All Sides, p. 341-342.

Appendix I
Claims Of Vietnamese Pilots

Pilots known to have claimed at the least one victory as individuals or in cooperation with others are identified by name in anglicized form and Vietnamese form and the number of official victories accredited is noted. Known claims of aerial victories, whether subsequently confirmed or not, are listed with the following information: the date of the claim, the aircraft type believed shot down, the unit served with when the claim was made, the aircraft in which the claim was made. Additional biographical information is noted. Footnotes include information in respect of the aircraft and crew attacked and, or, a listing of pilots who shared the claim.

Bui Dinh Kinh

Bùi Đinh Kinh

Official Victories: 2

Known Claims

29/04/1966	A-1[142]	921st F.R.	MiG-17
05/10/1966	F-4[143]	921st F.R.	MiG-21

Notes: served with the 921st Fighter Regiment, ejected on 05/11/1966, killed in action 10/08/1967, attained the rank of Captain.

Bui Doan Do

Bùi Doãn Độ

Official Victories: 1

---

[142] A-1E 52-132680, 602 ACS, 14 Air Commando Wing (ACW), USAF, Captain Leo S. Boston, killed in action.

[143] F-4C 64-0702, 433 TFS, 8 TFW, USAF, First Lieutenant Edward W. Garland (pilot), recovered, Captain William R. Andrews, killed in action.

Known Claims

29/12/1972	F-4	921st F.R.	MiG-21

Notes: trained in the USSR, served with the 921st Fighter Regiment, ejected on 08/01/1973, became a pilot with Vietnam Airlines.

Bui Duc Nhu

Bùi Đức Nhu

Official Victories: 3

See the biography and known claims listed under The Aces.

Bui Thanh Liem

Bùi Thanh Liêm

Official Victories: 2

Known Claims

10/06/1972	F-4[144]	921st F.R.	MiG-21
24/06/1972	AQM-34[145]	921st F.R.	MiG-21
27/06/1972	F-4[146]	921st F.R.	MiG-21
12/11/1972	AQM-34	921st F.R.	MiG-21

Notes: born on 30/06/1949 in Hai Ba Trung District, Hanoi, joined the military in February 1966, trained in the USSR, served with the 921st Fighter Regiment, ejected on 28/08/1972, married Nguyen Thi Tuyet, graduated from the Gagarin Air Force Academy in 1978, trained to be a

---

[144] A single VPAF claim was made and shared by Bui Than Liem and Pham Phu Thai.

[145] A single VPAF claim was made and shared by Bui Than Liem and Do Van Lanh.

[146] Either F-4E 69-7271, 4 TFS, 366 TFW, USAF, Captain Lynn A. Aikman (pilot), recovered, Captain Thomas J. Hanton, prisoner of war or F4E 69-7296, 390 TFS, 366 TFW, USAF, Major R. C. Miller (pilot), recovered, First Lieutenant Richard H. McDow, prisoner of war.

cosmonaut acting in reserve for Pham Tuan, killed in a flying accident while in a MiG-21UM on 22/09/1981, attained the rank of Major.

Bui Van Suu
Bùi Văn Sưu
Official Victories: 3

Known Claims

21/09/1967	F-4	923rd F.R.	MiG-17
06/11/1967	F-105[147]	923rd F.R.	MiG-17
17/12/1967	F-4[148]	923rd F.R.	Shenyang J-5 2037
03/01/1968	F-4[149]	923rd F.R.	Shenyang J-5 2037

Notes: born on 11/12/1943 in Dong Hung District, Thai Binh Province, trained in the USSR, served with the 923rd and 925th Fighter Regiments, left the military in 1993 and joined the Civil Aviation Administration of Vietnam, retired in 2004, made Hero of the Vietnam People's Armed Forces on 30 August 1995.

Cao Son Khao
Cao Sơn Khảo
Official Victories: 1

Known Claims

10/05/1972	F-4	921st F.R.	MiG-21

---

[147] Possibly F-105D 62-4286, 469 TFS, 388 TFW, USAF, Major Robert W. Hagerman, killed in action.

[148] Possibly F-4D 66-7774, 497 TFS, 8 TFW, USAF, Major Kenneth R. Fleenor (pilot), prisoner of war, First Lieutenant Terry L. Boyer, prisoner of war.

[149] A single VPAF claim was made and shared by Bui Van Suu and Luu Huy Chao.

Notes: born on 10/01/1945 in Y Yen District, Nam Dinh Province, served with the 910th Training Regiment and the 923rd and 921st Fighter Regiments, killed in action by friendly fire on 10/05/1972, attained the rank of Senior Lieutenant.

Cao Thanh Tinh

Cao Thanh Tịnh

Official Victories: 2

Known Claims

12/05/1967	3 F-4s[150]	923rd F.R.	MiG-17
23/08/1967	F-105	923rd F.R.	MiG-17

Note: served with the 921st and 923rd Fighter Regiments.

Dang Ngoc Ngu

Đặng Ngọc Ngự

Official Victories: 7

See the biography and known claims listed under The Aces.

Dinh Ton

Đinh Tôn

Official Victories: 4

---

[150] One of the claims was F-4C 63-7614, 390 TFS, 366 TFW, USAF, Colonel Norman C. Gaddis (pilot), prisoner of war, First Lieutenant James M. Jefferson, killed in action. One or both of the other claims may have been F-105D 59-1728, 357 TFS, 355 TFW, USAF, Captain Earl W. Grenzebach Jr., killed in action and, or, F-105F 63-8269 34 TFS, 388 TFW, USAF, Captain Peter P. Pitman (pilot), killed in action, Captain Robert A. Stewart, killed in action. Three VPAF claims were made and shared by Cao Than Thinh, Hoang Van Ky, Le Hai, Ngo Duc Mai and anti-aircraft units.

See the biography and known claims listed under The Aces.

Do Van Lanh
Đỗ Văn Lanh
Official Victories: 4

See the biography and known claims listed under The Aces.

Dong Van De
Đồng Văn Đe
Official Victories: 2

Known Claims
14/12/1966   2 F-105s[151]   921st F.R.   MiG-21

Notes: trained to fly the MiG-17 in the PRC, served with the 921st Fighter Regiment, trained to fly the MiG-21 in the DRV, killed in action on 06/01/1967, attained the rank of Senior Lieutenant.

Dong Van Song
Đồng Văn Song
Official Victories: 4

See the biography and known claims listed under The Aces.

Duong Ba Khang
Dương Bá Kháng
Official Victories: 2

---

[151] One of the claims was F-105D 60-0502, 357 TFS, 355 TFW, USAF, Captain Robert B. Cooley, recovered.

Known Claims

15/12/1972	AQM-34	927th F.R.	MiG-21
27/12/1972	F-4[152]	927th F.R.	MiG-21

Notes: born in Thua Thein-Hue Province, trained in the USSR, served with the 927th Fighter Regiment, attained the rank of Lieutenant Colonel.

Duong Trung Tan

Dương Trung Tân

Official Victories: 2

See the biography and known claims listed under The Aces.

Ha Dinh Bon

Hà Đinh Bôn

Official Victories: 1

Known Claims

25/04/1967	2 A-4s,		
	1 F-8 [153]	923rd F.R.	MiG-17

Notes: also known as Ha Bon, Hà Bôn, and as Nguyen Bon, Nguyễn Bôn, served with the 923rd Fighter Regiment, killed in action on 20/08/1967, attained the rank of Senior Lieutenant.

---

[152] Possibly F-4E 67-0292, 13 TFS. 432 TRW, USAF, Major Carl H. Jeffcoat (pilot), prisoner of war, First Lieutenant Jack R. Trimble, prisoner of war.

[153] One of the claims was A-4C 147799, VA-76, USN, Bon Homme Richard, Lieutenant Charles D. Stackhouse, prisoner of war. One of the claims was possibly A-4E 151116, VA-192, USN, USS Ticonderoga, Lieutenant Commander Francis J. Almberg, recovered. Three VPAF claims were made and shared by Ha Dinh Bon (Ha Bon, Nguyen Bon), Nguyen Ba Dich, Nguyen The Hon, Nguyen Van Bay.

Ha Quang Hung
Hà Quang Hưng
Official Victories: undetermined

Known Claims
04/07/1969   AQM-34[154] 921st F.R.   MiG-21

Notes: served with the 921st Fighter Regiment, ejected from MiG-21 flown after being hit by a Talos SAM fired from USS Long Beach on 23/05/1968.

Ha Van Chuc
Hà Văn Chúc
Official Victories: 2

Known Claims
03/01/1968   F-105[155]   921st F.R.   MiG-21
14/01/1968   F-105[156]   921st F.R.   MiG-21PFL 4320

Notes: born in 1938 in Lap Thach District, Vinh Yen Province, served with the 921st Fighter Regiment, ejected on 14/01/1968, died of wounds on 19/01/1968, attained the rank of Senior Lieutenant, made Hero of the Vietnam People's Armed Forces on 30 August 1995.

Ha Vinh Thanh
Hạ Vĩnh Thành
Official Victories: 1

---

[154] A single VPAF claim was made and shared by Ha Quang Hung and Nguyen Ngoc Thien.

[155] Possibly F-105D 58-1157, 469 TFS, 388 TFW, USAF, Colonel James E. Bean, prisoner of war.

[156] F-105D 60-0489, 469 TFS, 388 TFW, USAF, Major Stanley H. Horne, killed in action.

Known Claims

05/07/1972	F-4[157]	927th F.R.	MiG-21

Notes: born on 15/08/1947 in Bac Ninh Province, joined the military in 1965, trained in the USSR, served with the 923rd and 927th Fighter Regiments, attained the rank of Lieutenant Colonel prior to retiring from service in 1990, became a pilot with Vietnam Airlines.

Han Vinh Tuong
Hán Vĩnh Tưởng
Official Victories: 3

Known Claims

18/05/1972	F-4	923rd F.R.	MiG-17
11/07/1972	F-4	923rd F.R.	MiG-17
06/01/1973	AQM-34	927th F.R.	MiG-21

Notes: born in 1945 in Tam Nong District in Phu Tho Province, joined the military on 20/08/1965, trained in the PRC, served with the 923rd and 927th Fighter Regiments, graduated from the Military Political Academy and assumed many political roles in the VPAF, attained the rank of Lieutenant General prior to retiring from service in 2005, made Hero of the Vietnam People's Armed Forces on 10 August 2015.

Ho Van Quy
Hồ Văn Quỳ
Official Victories: 3

Known Claims

04/06/1965	F-4	921st F.R.	MiG-17
26/04/1966	2 F-4s	923rd F.R.	MiG-17

---

[157] Either F4E 67-0339, 34 TFS, 388 TFW, Major William J. Elander (pilot), prisoner of war, First Lieutenant Donald K. Logan, prisoner of war or F-4E 67-0296, 34 TFS, 388 TFW, USAF, Captain William A. Spencer (pilot), prisoner of war, First Lieutenant Brian J. Seek, prisoner of war.

21/09/1967   F-4   923rd F.R.   MiG-17

Notes: was born in 1935 in Thang Binh District, Quang Nam Province, trained in the PRC, served with the 921st, 923rd and 925th Fighter Regiments, attained the rank of Colonel, made Hero of the Vietnam People's Armed Forces on 10 August 2015.

Hoang Bieu
Hoàng Biểu
Official Victories: 2

Known Claims
14/12/1966	AQM-34[158]	921st F.R.	MiG-21
23/02/1968	F-4[159]	921st F.R.	MiG-21
13/07/1969	AQM-34	921st F.R.	MiG-21

Notes: trained in the USSR, served with the 921st Fighter Regiment, ejected on 30/03/1972, retired from service in 2001.

Hoang Cao Bong
Hoàng Cao Bổng
Official Victories: 1

Known Claims
undetermined   F-4   925th F.R.   MiG-19

Notes: was born 17/08/1942 in Tien Hai District, Thai Binh Province, joined the military in February 1964, trained in the PRC, served with the 925th

---

[158] A single VPAF claim was made and shared by Hoang Bieu and Pham Than Ngan.

[159] F-4D, 66-8725, 497 TFS, 8 TFW, USAF, Major Laird Gutterson (pilot), prisoner of war, First Lieutenant Myron L. Donald, prisoner of war. A single VPAF claim was made and shared by Hoang Bieu and pilots of the DPRK of Group Z flying MiG-21s of the 921st Fighter Regiment.

Fighter Regiment, attained the rank of Colonel prior to retiring from service in 1999.

Hoang Cong
Hoàng Cống
Official Victories: 1

Known Claims
26/06/1969   AQM-34   923rd F.R.   MiG-17
03/08/1969   AQM-34[160] 923rd F.R.   MiG-17
Notes: served with the 923rd Fighter Regiment, killed in action on 08/01/1973, attained the rank of Captain.

Hoang Ich
Hoàng Ích
Official Victories: 1

Known Claims
date, type undetermined   923rd F.R.   MiG-17

Notes: served with the 923rd Fighter Regiment, killed in action 06/03/1972.

Hoang Mai Vuong
Hoàng Mai Vượng
Official Victories: 1

Known Claims
08/01/1973   AQM-34   923rd F.R.   MiG-17

---

[160] A single VPAF claim was made and shared by Hoang Cong and Le Hai.

Notes: born in 1947 in Dien Chau in Nghe An, trained in the USSR, served with the 923rd Fighter Regiment, participated in the attack on the Tan Son Nhat airbase flying an A-37 on 28/04/1975, killed in a flying accident 15/07/1975, attained the rank of Senior Lieutenant, made Hero of the Vietnam People's Armed Forces on 9 July 2014.

Hoang Quoc Dung
Hoàng Quốc Dũng
Official Victories: 1

Known Claims
27/04/1972   F-4[161]   921st F.R.   MiG-21

Notes: born on 10/08/1945 in Dien Ban District, Quang Nam Province, joined the military in June 1965, served with the 921st Fighter Regiment, studied at the Gagarin Air Force Academy, attained the rank of Colonel prior to retiring from service in 2009.

Hoang Tam Hung
Hoàng Tam Hùng
Official Victories: 2

Known Claims
28/12/1972   1 RA-5[162],
                1 F-4   927th F.R.   MiG-21PFM 5013

Notes: born in Thua Thien-Hue Province, trained in the USSR, served with the 927th Fighter Regiment, killed in action flying MiG-21PFM 5013 on

---

[161] F-4B 153025, VF-51, USN, USS Coral Sea, Lieutenant Albert R. Molinare (pilot), prisoner of war, Lieutenant Commander James B. Souder, prisoner of war.

[162] RA-5C 156633, Navy Heavy Reconnaissance Attack Squadron, USN, USS Enterprise, Lieutenant Commander Alfred H. Agnew (pilot), prisoner of war, Lieutenant Michael F. Haifley, killed in action.

28/12/1972, attained the rank of Senior Lieutenant, made Hero of the Vietnam People's Armed Forces.

Hoang Van Ky
Hoàng Văn Kỷ
Official Victories: 4

See the biography and known claims listed under The Aces.

Lam Van Lich
Lâm Văn Lích
Official Victories: 3

Known Claims

17/06/1965	F-4	921st F.R.	MiG-17
03/02/1966	2 A-1s	921st F.R.	MiG-17PF 4721

Notes: born in 1932 in Gia Rai District, Bac Lieu Province, trained in the PRC, served with the 921st and 923rd Fighter Regiments, among the initial group of pilots to land at Phuc Yen on 06/08/1964, attained the rank of Colonel, made Hero of the Vietnam People's Armed Forces on 1 January 1967, died in 2014.

Le Hai
Lê Hải
Official Victories: 6

See the biography and known claims listed under The Aces.

Le Hong Diep
Lẽ Hồng Diệp
Official Victories: undetermined

Known Claims
23/08/1967   F-4[163]   923rd F.R.   MiG-17

Notes: also know as Nguyen Hong Diep, Nguyễn Hồng Diệp, served with the 923rd Fighter Regiment, ejected on 03/01/1968.

Le Minh Duong
Lê Minh Dương
Official Victories: undetermined

Known Claims
18/12/1971   F-4[164]   921st F.R.   MiG-21

Note: served with the 921st Fighter Regiment.

Le Minh Huan
Lê Minh Huân
Official Victories: 1

Known Claims
04/04/1965   F-105[165]   921st F.R.   Shenyang J-5 1036

---

[163] A single VPAF claim was made and shared by Le Hong Diep and Nguyen Van Tho.

[164] Possibly F-4D 64-0954, 13 TFS, 432 TRW, USAF, First Lieutenant Kenneth R. Wells (pilot), prisoner of war, Major Leland L. Hildebrand, prisoner of war. A single VPAF claim was made and shared by Le Minh Duong and Nguyen Van Khanh.

[165] F-105D 59-1754, 354 TFS, 355 TFW attached to 2 Air Division, USAF, Major Frank E. Bennett, killed in action.

Notes: served with the 921st Fighter Regiment, killed in action on 04/04/1965, attained the rank of Senior Lieutenant, made Hero of the Vietnam People's Armed Forces.

Le Quang Trung

Lê Quang Trung

Official Victories: 5

See the biography and known claims listed under The Aces.

Le Sy Diep

Lê Sỹ Diệp

Official Victories: 1

Known Claims

| 01/05/1967 | F-4 | 923rd F.R. | MiG-17 |

Notes: served with the 923rd Fighter Regiment, ejected on 26/10/1967, killed in action 29/07/1968, attained the rank of Senior Lieutenant.

Le Thanh Dao

Lê Thanh Đạo

Official Victories: 6

See the biography and known claims listed under The Aces.

Le Trong Huyen

Lê Trọng Huyên

Official Victories: 4

See the biography and known claims listed under The Aces.

Le Trong Long
Lê Trọng Long
Official Victories: 1

Known Claims
17/06/1965   F-4   921st F.R.   MiG-17

Notes: served with the 921st Fighter Regiment, killed in action on 17/06/1965, attained the rank of Senior Lieutenant.

Le Van Tuong
Lê Văn Tưởng
Official Victories: 1

Known Claims
10/05/1972   F-4[166]   925th F.R.   MiG-19

Notes: born in 1948, joined the military in July 1965, trained in the PRC, served with the 925th Fighter Regiment, killed in a flying accident attempting to land, the MiG-19 flown, without fuel on 10/05/1972, attained the rank of Lieutenant.

Le Xuan Dy
Lê Xuân Dỵ
Official Victories: 1

Known Claims
05/10/1967   A-4   923rd F.R.   MiG-17

Notes: born in 1938 in Tu Song District, Bac Ninh Province, trained in the USSR, served with the 923rd Fighter Regiment, participated in the attack on the 7th Fleet on 19/04/1972 flying MiG-17F 2019 causing significant damage to the USS Higbee, attained the rank of Colonel prior to retiring

---

[166] F-4E 67-0386, 58 TFS, 432 TRW, USAF, Captain Jeffrey L. Harris, killed in action (pilot), Captain Dennis E. Wilkinson, killed in action.

from service in 1998, made Hero of the Vietnam People's Armed Forces in 2015.

Luong The Phuc

Lương Thế Phúc
Official Victories: 1

Known Claims
09/09/1972   F-4[167]   921st F.R.   MiG-21

Notes: born on 27/09/1948, served with the 921st Fighter Regiment, ejected on 09/09/1972, became director of Vietnam Air Force Academy, retiring from service 1992, Standing Deputy General Director of Vietnam Airlines Corporation 1993 to 2009, Chairman of the Board of Directors of Jetstar Pacific Airlines Aviation Joint Stock Company between 1996 and 2005, became Deputy General Director and Member of the Board of Directors of VietJet Aviation Joint Stock Company in 2011.

Luong Xuan Truong

Lương Xuân Trường
Official Victories: 1

Known Claims
09/03/1971   AQM-34   923rd F.R.   MiG-17

Notes: served with the 923rd Fighter Regiment., killed in action on 09/03/1971, attained the rank of Lieutenant.

---

[167] F4E 69-7565, 307 TFS, 31 TFW attached to 432 TRW, USAF, Captain William J. Dalecky (pilot), recovered, Captain Terry M. Murphy, recovered. A single VPAF claim was made and shared by Do Van Lanh and Luong The Phuc.

Luu Huy Chao

Lưu Huy Chao

Official Victories: 6

See the biography and known claims listed under The Aces.

Mai Duc Toai

Mai Đức Toại

Official Victories: 2

Known Claims

16/08/1966	A-4	923rd F.R.	MiG-17
24/04/1967	F-105[168]	923rd F.R.	MiG-17
25/04/1967	F-105[169]	923rd F.R.	MiG-17

Notes: fought at Dien Bien Phu with the 130th Battalion, 209th Regiment, 312th Division, trained in the PRC, served with the 921st, 923rd and 925th Fighter Regiments, was the commander of the 925th Fighter Regiment between 1970 and 1973.

Mai Van Cuong

Mai Văn Cương

Official Victories: 8

See the biography and known claims listed under The Aces.

---

[168] A single VPAF claim was made and shared by Hoang Van Ky, Le Hai, Luu Huy Chao, Mai Duc Toai.

[169] F-105D 62-4294, 354 TFS, 355 TFW, USAF, First Lieutenant Robert L. Weskamp, killed in action. A single VPAF claim was made and shared by Hoang Van Ky, Le Hai, Luu Huy Chao, Mai Duc Toai.

Nghiem Dinh Hieu
Nghiêm Đinh Hi`êu
Official Victories: 1

Known Claims
date, type undetermined   921st F.R.   MiG

Notes: served with the 921st Fighter Regiment, ejected from MiG-21PFL 4024 on 20/05/1967, died of wounds on 20/05/1967, attained the rank of Lieutenant.

Ngo Doan Nhung
Ngô Đoàn Nhung
Official Victories: 1

Known Claims
06/11/1965   CH-3[170]   921st F.R.   MiG-17

Notes: born in 1940, served with the 921st and 923rd Fighter Regiments, killed in action on 21/11/1967, attained the rank of Senior Lieutenant.

Ngo Duc Mai
Ngô Đức Mai
Official Victories: 3

See the biography and known claims listed under The Aces.

---

[170] CH-3C 63-09685, 38 ARRS, USAF, Captain Warren R. Lilly (pilot), prisoner of war, First Lieutenant Jerry A. Singleton, prisoner of war, Staff Sergeant Berkley E. Naugle, recovered, Staff Sergeant Arthur Cormier, prisoner of war. A single VPAF claim was made and shared by Ngo Doan Nhung, Pham Ngoc Lan, Tran Hanh, Tran Minh Phuong.

Ngo Duy Thu

Ngô Duy Thư

Official Victories: 3

Known Claims

11/05/1972	F-105[171]	927th F.R.	MiG-21
24/06/1972	F-4	927th F.R.	MiG-21
27/06/1972	F-4[172]	927th F.R.	MiG-21

Notes: born in 1947 in Nam Truc District, Nam Dinh Province, trained in the USSR, served with the 923rd, 921st and 927th Fighter Regiments, ejected on 16/09/1972, studied at the Gagarin Air Force Academy, killed in a flying accident on 29/11/1978, attained the rank of Captain, made Hero of the Vietnam People's Armed Forces on 9 October 2014 .

Ngo Son

Ngô Sơn

Official Victories: 1

Known Claims

27/07/1970	AQM-34	923rd F.R.	MiG-17

Notes: born on 15/06/1942 in Phu Cu District, Hung Yen Province, trained in the USSR, served with the 923rd Fighter Regiment, attained the rank of Colonel prior to retiring from service in 1993.

---

[171] F-105G 62-4424, 17 Wild Weasel Squadron, 388 TFW, USAF, Major William H. Talley (pilot), prisoner of war, Major James P. Padgett, prisoner of war.

[172] Possibly F-4E 68-0314, 308 TFS, 31 TFW attached to 432 TRW, USAF, Lieutenant Colonel Farrell J. Sullivan (pilot), killed in action, Captain Richard L. Francis, prisoner of war.

Ngo Van Phu

Ngô Văn Phú

Official Victories: 1

Known Claims:

11/05/1972   F-4[173]   927th F.R.   MiG-21

Notes: born in Kim Dong District in Hung Yen Province, trained in the USSR, served with the 921st and 927th Fighter Regiments, ejected on 11/05/1972, studied at the Gagarin Air Force Academy.

Nguyen Ba Dich

Nguyễn Bá Địch

Official Victories: 3

See the biography and known claims listed under The Aces.

Nguyen Cong Huy

Nguyễn Công Huy

Official Victories: 1

Known Claims

26/06/1972   F-4   921st F.R.   MiG-21

Notes: born on 18/05/1947 in Thuong Tin District, Ha Tay Province, trained in the USSR, served with the 921st Fighter Regiment, ejected on 12/08/1972, studied at the Gagarin Air Force Academy, attained the rank of Colonel, became an author.

---

[173] F-4D 66-0230, 555 TFS, 432 TRW, USAF, Lieutenant Colonel Joseph W. Kittinger II (pilot), prisoner of war, First Lieutenant William J. Reich, prisoner of war.

Nguyen Dang Kinh

Nguyễn Đăng Kỉnh

Official Victories: 6

See the biography and known claims listed under The Aces.

Nguyen Dinh Phuc

Nguyễn Đinh Phúc

Official Victories: 3

Known Claims

05/06/1967	F-105	923rd F.R.	MiG-17
06/11/1967	F-105[174]	923rd F.R.	MiG-17
19/11/1967	F-4	923rd F.R.	MiG-17
14/12/1967	F-8[175]	923rd F.R.	MiG-17

Notes: served with the 923rd Fighter Regiment, killed in action on 14/12/1967, attained the rank of Senior Lieutenant.

Nguyen Duc Soat

Nguyễn Đức Soát

Official Victories: 6

See the biography and known claims listed under The Aces.

Nguyen Duc Thuan

Nguyễn Đức Thuận

Official Victories: 2

---

[174] Possibly F-105D 62-4286, 469 TFS, 388 TFW, USAF, Major Robert W. Hagerman, killed in action.

[175] A single VPAF claim was made and shared by Luu Huy Chao and Nguyen Dinh Phuc.

Known Claims

| 13/12/1966 | F-105[176] | 921st F.R. | MiG-21 |
| 03/03/1968 | AQM-34 | 921st F.R. | MiG-21 |

Notes: served with the 921st Fighter Regiment, ejected on 02/01/1967.

Nguyen Hong My
Nguyễn Hồng Mỹ
Official Victories: 1

Known Claims

| 19/01/1972 | F-4[177] | 921st F.R. | MiG-21PFM 5018 |

Notes: born in 1946 in Nam Dan District, Nghe An Province, joined the military on 01/07/1965, trained in the USSR, served with the 921st Fighter Regiment, participated in the memorial flight for Ho Chi Minh on 09/09/1969, presented with the Uncle Ho badge for the victory of 19/01/1972 by Vo Nguyen Giap personally, ejected from MiG-21MF 5112 and wounded in action on 16/04/1972.

Nguyen Hong Nhi
Nguyễn Hồng Nhị
Official Victories: 8

See the biography and known claims listed under The Aces.

---

[176] F-105D 61-0187, 421 TFS, 388 TFW, USAF, Captain Samuel E. Waters, killed in action.

[177] Possibly RF-4C 68-0573, 14 TRS, 432 TRW, USAF, Major Robert K. Mock (pilot), recovered, First Lieutenant John L. Stiles, recovered. VPAF records indicate the claim was made on 19/01/1972 while USAF records indicate the loss occurred on 20/01/1972, however, Nguyen Hong My and John L. Stiles agreed that the claim and the loss were one and the same despite the discrepancy when interviewed by John Mollison.

Nguyen Hong Son
Nguyễn Hồng Sơn
Official Victories: 1

Known Claims

23/05/1972   F-4[178]   925th F.R.   Shenyang J-6 6026

Note: served with the 925th Fighter Regiment.

Nguyen Hung Son
Nguyễn Hùng Sơn
Official Victories: 1

Known Claims

08/05/1972   F-4   925th F.R.   Shenyang J-6 6029

Notes: born on 22/06/1947, served with the 925th Fighter Regiment, ejected on 11/06/1972, attained the rank of Senior Colonel.

Nguyen Huu Tao
Nguyễn Hữu Tào
Official Victories: 1

Known Claims

12/08/1967   F-4   923rd F.R.   MiG-17
25/10/1967   F-105[179] 923rd F.R.   MiG-17

Notes: born in 1933 in Dien Ban District, Quang Nam Province, joined the military in 1949, trained in the PRC, served with the 923rd Fighter

---

[178] A single VPAF claim was made and shared by Nguyen Hong Son and Pham Hung Son.

[179] F-105D 59-1735, 333 TFS, 355 TFW, USAF, Captain Ramon A. Horinek, prisoner of war.

Regiment, ejected and killed in action on 06/11/1967, attained the rank of Captain.

Nguyen Khac Loc
Nguyễn Khắc Lộc
Official Victories: 1

Known Claims
23/04/1966   F-4   923rd F.R.   MiG-17
Notes: served with the 923rd Fighter Regiment, ejected on 29/04/1966 and wounded in action then wandered through forest for 10 days before being found.

Nguyen Ngoc Do
Nguyễn Ngọc Độ
Official Victories: 6

See the biography and known claims listed under The Aces.

Nguyen Ngoc Hung
Nguyễn Ngọc Hưng
Official Victories: 1

Known Claims
18/05/1972   F-4   927th F.R.   MiG-21

Notes: served with the 921st and 927th Fighter Regiments, killed in action on 08/07/1972, attained the rank of Senior Lieutenant.

Nguyen Ngoc Thien
Nguyễn Ngọc Thiện
Official Victories: undetermined

Known Claims
04/07/1969   AQM-34[180] 921st F.R.   MiG-21

Notes: served with the 921st Fighter Regiment, killed in action on 10/08/1972, attained the rank of Senior Lieutenant.

Nguyen Ngoc Tiep
Nguyễn Ngọc Tiếp
Official Victories: 1

Known Claims
08/05/1972   F-4   925th F.R.   Shenyang J-6 6005

Notes: born in 1942, served with the 925th Fighter Regiment, killed in a flying accident on 15/08/1975, attained the rank of Senior Lieutenant.

Nguyen Nhat Chieu
Nguyễn Nhật Chiêu
Official Victories: 6

See the biography and known claims listed under The Aces.

Nguyen Phi Hung
Nguyễn Phi Hùng
Official Victories: 5

See the biography and known claims listed under The Aces.

---

[180] A single VPAF claim was made and shared by Ha Quang Hung and Nguyen Ngoc Thien.

Nguyen Phu Ninh

Nguyễn Phú Ninh

Official Victories: 1

Known Claims

| 25/10/1967 | F-4 | 923rd F.R. | MiG-17 |

Note: served with the 923rd Fighter Regiment.

Nguyen Quang Sinh

Nguyễn Quang Sinh

Official Victories: 2

Known Claims

| 05/06/1967 | F-105 | 923rd F.R. | MiG-17 |

Notes: served with the 923rd Fighter Regiment, killed in a flying accident on 04/03/1969, attained the rank of Senior Lieutenant.

Nguyen Thanh Xuan

Nguyễn Thanh Xuân

Official Victories: 1

Known Claims

| 08/06/1972 | F-4 | 927th F.R. | MiG-21 |

Notes: served with the 927th Fighter Regiment, ejected from MiG-21PFM 5034 on 29/07/1972.

Nguyen The Hon

Nguyễn Thế Hôn

Official Victories: 3

See the biography and known claims listed under The Aces.

Nguyen Tien Sam
Nguyễn Tiến Sâm
Official Victories: 5

See the biography and known claims listed under The Aces.

Nguyen Van Ba
Nguyễn Văn Ba
Official Victories: 1

Known Claims:
16/02/1964   C-123[181]   919 A.T.R.   T-28D 963

Notes: Born in 1930 in Mo Cay District, Ben Tre Province, served with the 919th Air Transport Regiment, claimed the first victory of the VPAF flying with Le Tien Phuoc on 16/02/1964, died of cardiovascular disease on 14/09/1996, made Hero of the Vietnam People's Armed Forces.

Nguyen Van Bay
Nguyễn Văn Bảy
Official Victories: 7

See the biography and known claims listed under The Aces.

Nguyen Van Bay
Nguyễn Văn Bảy
Official Victories: undetermined

---

[181] Possibly a C-123 of the VNAF.

Known Claims

06/05/1972	A-6	923rd F.R.	MiG-17

Notes: born in 1943 in Bac Lieu Province, trained in the USSR, served with the 923rd Fighter Regiment, participated in the attack on the 7th Fleet on 19/04/1972 flying MiG-17F 2047 causing slight damage to the USS Oklahoma City, killed in action 06/05/1972, attained the rank of Lieutenant, made Hero of the Vietnam People's Armed Forces on 20/12/1994.

Nguyen Van Bien
Nguyễn Văn Biên
Official Victories: 2

Known Claims

19/07/1966	F-105[182]	923rd F.R.	MiG-17
29/09/1966	AQM-34	923rd F.R.	MiG-17

Notes: served with the 923rd Fighter Regiment, killed in action on 29/09/1966, attained the rank of Captain.

Nguyen Van Coc
Nguyễn Văn Cốc
Official Victories: 9

See the biography and known claims listed under The Aces.

Nguyen Van Dien
Nguyễn Văn Điển
Official Victories: 1

---

[182] Possibly F-105D 60-5382, 354 TFS, 355 TFW, USAF, Captain Richard E. Steere, recovered.

Known Claims
23/05/1972   F-4[183]   923rd F.R.   MiG-17

Notes: served with the 923rd Fighter Regiment, killed in action on 23/05/1972, attained the rank of Lieutenant.

Nguyen Van Khanh
Nguyễn Văn Khánh
Official Victories: undetermined

Known Claims
03/07/1968   AQM-34[184] 921st F.R.   MiG-21
20/02/1969   AQM-34   921st F.R.   MiG-21
18/12/1971   F-4[185]   921st F.R.   MiG-21

Notes: served with the 921st Fighter Regiment, participated in the memorial flypast for Ho Chi Minh on 09/09/1969, killed in action by friendly fire on 18/12/1971, attained the rank of Senior Lieutenant.

Nguyen Van Lai
Nguyễn Văn Lai
Official Victories: 2

Known Claims
20/06/1965   2 A-1s   921st F.R.   MiG-17

---

[183] A single VPAF claim was made and shared by Nguyen Van Dien and Vu Van Dang.

[184] A single VPAF claim was made and shared by Nguyen Van Khanh and Nguyen Van Ly.

[185] Possibly F-4D 64-0954, 13 TFS, 432 TRW, USAF, First Lieutenant Kenneth R. Wells (pilot), prisoner of war, Major Leland L. Hildebrand, prisoner of war. A single VPAF claim was made and shared by Le Minh Duong and Nguyen Van Khanh.

Notes: trained in the PRC, served with the 921st Fighter Regiment, killed in action on 20/06/1965, attained the rank of Lieutenant.

Nguyen Van Luc
Nguyễn Văn Lục
Official Victories: 3

Known Claims

09/12/1968	AQM-34	923rd F.R.	MiG-17
15/12/1968	AQM-34	923rd F.R.	MiG-17
06/05/1972	A-6	923rd F.R.	MiG-17

Notes: served with the 923rd Fighter Regiment, named commander of the the Invincible Flight and as such participated in the attack on the Tan Son Nhat airbase flying an A-37 on 28/04/1975.

Nguyen Van Lung
Nguyễn Văn Lung
Official Victories: 1

Known Claims

27/05/1968	AQM-34[186]	921st F.R.	MiG-21
12/10/1968	AQM-34	921st F.R.	MiG-21

Notes: served with the 921st and 927th Fighter Regiments, killed in action on 31/05/1972, attained the rank of Senior Lieutenant.

Nguyen Van Ly
Nguyễn Văn Lý
Official Victories: 3

---

[186] A single VPAF claim was made and shared by Bui Duc Nhu and Nguyen Van Lung.

Known Claims

05/06/1967	F-105	921st F.R.	MiG-21
17/07/1967	F-8	921st F.R.	MiG-21
03/07/1968	AQM-34[187]	921st F.R.	MiG-21

Notes: trained in the USSR, served with the 921st Fighter Regiment, known to have flown MiG-21PFL 4324, ejected from MiG-21 flown after being hit by a Talos SAM fired from USS Long Beach on 22/09/1968, participated in the memorial flypast for Ho Chi Minh leading the 2nd flight over Ba Dinh square on 09/09/1969.

Nguyen Van Minh
Nguyễn Văn Minh
Official Victories: 3

Known Claims

09/10/1966	2 F-4s[188]	921st F.R.	MiG-21PFL 4221
17/08/1968	F-4[189]	921st F.R.	MiG-21

Notes: born on 02/07/1939 in Xuan Truong District, Nam Dinh Province, joined the military in February 1960, trained in the USSR, served with the 921st Fighter Regiment, ejected from MiG-21PFL 4221 on 09/10/1966 and wounded in action, made Hero of the Vietnam People's Armed Forces in 2018.

---

[187] A single VPAF claim was made and shared by Nguyen Van Khanh and Nguyen Van Ly.

[188] One of the claims was F-4B 152993, VF-154, USN, USS Coral Sea, Lieutenant Commander Charles N. Tanner (pilot), prisoner of war, Lieutenant Ross R. Terry, prisoner of war.

[189] Possibly F-4B 151404 VF-142, USN, USS Constellation, Lieutenant (Junior Grade) Markham L. Gartley, (pilot), prisoner of war, Lieutenant William J. Mayhew, prisoner of war.

Nguyen Van Nghia
Nguyễn Văn Nghĩa
Official Victories: 5

See the biography and known claims listed under The Aces.

Nguyen Van Nhuong
Nguyễn Văn Nhượng
Official Victories: 1

Known Claims
04/01/1973   AQM-34   927th F.R.   MiG-21

Note: served with the 927th Fighter Regiment.

Nguyen Van Phi
Nguyễn Văn Phi
Official Victories: 1

Known Claims
13/05/1967   F-105   923rd F.R.   MiG-17

Notes: served with the 923rd Fighter Regiment, killed in action on 19/05/1967, attained the rank of Senior Lieutenant.

Nguyen Van Phuc
Nguyễn Văn Phúc
Official Victories: 1

Known Claims
10/05/1972   F-4[190]   925th F.R.   MiG-19

---

[190] F-4D 65-0784, 555 TFS, 432 TRW, USAF, Major Robert A. Lodge (pilot), killed in action, Captain Roger C. Locher, recovered.

Notes: born in 1946 in Y Yen District, Nam Dinh Province, joined the military in August 1965, trained in the PRC, served with the 925th Fighter Regiment, killed in action 11/06/1972, attained the rank of Lieutenant.

Nguyen Van Tho
Nguyễn Văn Thọ
Official Victories: 1

Known Claims

19/04/1967	A-1[191]	923rd F.R.	MiG-17
12/05/1967	F-105[192]	923rd F.R.	MiG-17
23/08/1967	F-4[193]	923rd F.R.	MiG-17
06/11/1967	F-105	923rd F.R.	MiG-17

Notes: born on 16/10/1943 in Phu My District, Binh Dinh Province, served with the 923rd and 927th Fighter Regiments, ejected on 10/05/1972, organized the training of the Invincible Flight on the A-37, attained the rank of Colonel.

Nguyen Van Toan
Nguyễn Văn Toàn
Official Victories: 2

Known Claims

24/06/1972	F-4	927th F.R.	MiG-21
26/08/1972	F-4	927th F.R.	MiG-21

---

[191] A-1E, 52-133905, 602 ACS, 56 ACW, USAF, Major John S. Hamilton, killed in action.

[192] Possibly F-105D 59-1728, 357 TFS, 355 TFW, USAF, Captain Earl W. Grenzebach, killed in action.

[193] A single VPAF claim was made and shared by Le Hong Diep and Nguyen Van Tho.

Notes: served with the 927th Fighter Regiment, ejected on 12/09/1972.

Nguyen Van Va
Nguyễn Văn Va
Official Victories: undetermined

Known Claims
26/08/1972   AQM-34   923rd F.R.   MiG-17

Note: served with the 923rd Fighter Regiment.

Pham Dinh Tuan
Phạm Đinh Tuân
Official Victories: 1

Known Claims
28/01/1970   F-4   921st F.R.   MiG-21

Notes: served with the 921st Fighter Regiment, participated in the memorial flypast for Ho Chi Minh on 09/09/1969, killed in action on 28/01/1970, attained the rank of Lieutenant.

Pham Hung Son
Phạm Hùng Sơn
Official Victories: 1

Known Claims
23/05/1972   F-4[194]   925th F.R.   MiG-19

Notes: born on 23/09/1946 in Ha Tay Province, trained in the PRC, served with the 925th Fighter Regiment, studied at the Gagarin Air Force

[194] A single VPAF claim was made and shared by Nguyen Hong Son and Pham Hung Son.

Academy, attained the rank of Colonel prior to retiring from service in 2007 .

Pham Ngoc Lan

Phạm Ngọc Lan
Official Victories: 1

Known Claims

03/04/1965	F-8[195]	921st F.R.	Shenyang J-5 2310
06/11/1965	CH-3[196]	921st F.R.	Shenyang J-5 2050

Notes: born on 19/02/1934 in Dien Ban District, Quang Nam Province, joined the military in July 1952, trained in the PRC between 1956 and 1964, served with the 921st Fighter Regiment, among the initial group of pilots to land at Phuc Yen on 06/08/1964, became the first pilot of a Fighter Regiment to claim a victory then without fuel made an emergency landing along the Duong River on 03/04/1965, ejected on 06/11/1966, studied at the Gagarin Air Force Academy, became the Director of the Training Department Of The Air Force Military School in 1985, attained the rank of Major General prior to retiring from service in 1999, died in June 2019 in Hanoi, made Hero of the Vietnam People's Armed Forces on 28 May 2010.

Pham Ngoc Tam

Phạm Ngọc Tâm
Official Victories: 1

---

[195] F-8E 150845, damaged, VF-211, USN, USS Hancock, Lieutenant Commander Spence Thomas.

[196] CH-3C 63-09685, 38 ARRS, USAF, Captain Warren R. Lilly (pilot), prisoner of war, First Lieutenant Jerry A. Singleton, prisoner of war, Staff Sergeant Berkley E. Naugle, recovered, Staff Sergeant Arthur Cormier, prisoner of war. A single VPAF claim was made and shared by Ngo Doan Nhung, Pham Ngoc Lan, Tran Hanh, Tran Minh Phuong.

Known Claims
18/05/1972   F-4[197]   925th F.R.   MiG-19

Notes: born in 1943 in Phu My District, Binh Dinh Province, trained in the PRC, served with the 925th Fighter Regiment, ejected 18/05/1972, killed in action on 27/06/1972, attained the rank of Senior Lieutenant.

Pham Phu Thai
Phạm Phú Thái
Official Victories: 4

See the biography and known claims listed under The Aces.

Pham Thanh Chung
Phạm Thành Chung
Official Victories: 1

Known Claims
21/06/1966   1 RF-8[198]
                1 F-8   923rd F.R.   MiG-17
14/07/1966   A-4   923rd F.R.   MiG-17

Notes: served with the 923rd Fighter Regiment, killed in action by friendly fire on 18/08/1966, attained the rank of Captain.

---

[197] F-4D 66-7612, 421 TFS, 366 TFW, USAF, First Lieutenant Wesley D. Ratzel (pilot), killed in action, First Lieutenant Jonathan B. Bednarek, killed in action.

[198] One of the claims was possibly RF-8A 146830, Detachment L, VFP-63, USN, USS Hancock, Lieutenant Leonard C. Eastman, prisoner of war. One of the claims was F-8E 149152, VF-211, USN, USS Hancock, Lieutenant Commander Cole Black, prisoner of war. Two VPAF claims were made and shared by Duong Truong Tan, Nguyen Van Bay, Pham Thanh Chung, Phan Van Tuc.

Pham Thanh Nam
Phạm Thành Nam
Official Victories: 1

Known Claims
31/10/1968   AQM-34   921st F.R.   MiG-21
03/08/1969   AQM-34[199] 921st F.R.   MiG-21

Notes: served with the 921st Fighter Regiment, participated in the memorial flypast for Ho Chi Minh on 09/09/1969, killed in action on 28/03/1970, attained the rank of Lieutenant.

Pham Thanh Ngan
Phạm Thanh Ngân
Official Victories: 8

See the biography and known claims listed under The Aces.

Pham Tuan
Phạm Tuân
Official Victories: 1

Known Claims
27/12/1972   B-52[200]   921st F.R.   MiG-21MF 5121

Notes: born on 14/02/1947 in Kien Xuong District, Thai Binh Province, joined the military in September 1965, trained in the USSR between 1965

---

[199] One VPAF claim was made and shared by Nguyen Van Coc and Pham Thanh Nam.

[200] Possibly B-52D 56-0605, 7 Bombardment Wing attached to 43 Strategic Wing, USAF, Captain Frank D. Lewis (pilot), prisoner of war, Captain Samuel B. Cusimano, prisoner of war, Major James C. Condon, prisoner of war, Major Allen L. Johnson, killed in action, First Lieutenant Bennie L. Fryer, killed in action, Master Sergeant James W. Gough, prisoner of war.

and 1968, served with the 923rd and 921st Fighter Regiments, married Tran Phuong Tan, studied at the Gagarin Air Force Academy, trained to be a cosmonaut, left earth aboard Soyuz-37 on 23/07/1980 with Viktor Gorbatko, docked with Salyut-6 on 24/07/1980, conducted numerous experiments in space, returned to earth aboard Soyuz-36 on 31/07/1980 with Gorbatko, attained the rank of Lieutenant General prior to retiring from service in 2008, made Hero of the Vietnam People's Armed Forces on 3 September 1973, Hero of Labour on 1 August 1980 and Hero of the Soviet Union and awarded the Order of Lenin on 31 July 1980.

Phan Diet

Phan Điệt

Official Victories: 1

Known Claims
19/05/1967   F-4   923rd F.R.   MiG-17

Notes: also know as Nguyen Huu Diet, Nguyễn Hữu Điệt, served with the 923rd Fighter Regiment, ejected on 19/05/1967.

Phan Thanh Nha

Phan Thanh Nhạ

Official Victories: 1

Known Claims
10/07/1965   F-4   921st F.R.   MiG-17

Notes: served with the 921st Fighter Regiment, killed in action on 10/07/1965, attained the rank of Senior Lieutenant.

Phan Thanh Tai

Phan Thanh Tài

Official Victories: 2

Known Claims

28/04/1967	F-105	923rd F.R.	MiG-17
19/05/1967	F-4	923rd F.R.	MiG-17

Notes: served with the 921st Fighter Regiment, killed in action on 19/05/1967, attained the rank of Senior Lieutenant.

Phan Trong Van
Phan Trọng Vân

Official Victories: 1

Known Claims

12/05/1967	F-105	923rd F.R.	MiG-17
19/09/1967	F-105	923rd F.R.	MiG-17

Notes: served with the 923rd and the 925th Fighter Regiments, ejected on 12/05/1967, ejected on 06/11/1967, killed in action by friendly fire on 02/06/1972, attained the rank of Captain.

Phan Van Na
Phan Văn Na

Official Victories: 1

Known Claims

13/07/1966	A-4	923rd F.R.	MiG-17

Note: served with the 923rd Fighter Regiment.

Phan Van Tuc
Phan Văn Túc

Official Victories: 4

See the biography and known claims listed under The Aces.

Phung Van Quang
Phùng Văn Quảng
Official Victories: 1

Known Claims
02/09/1972   F-105   925th F.R.   Shenyang J-6 6024

Notes: born in Hung Yen Province, served with the 925th Fighter Regiment, joined the Civil Aviation Administration of Vietnam, became the Chief Administrator of the National Committee of Air Search and Rescue.

To Nhat Bai
To Nhất Bài
Official Victories: undetermined

Known Claims
19/01/1973   AQM-34   923rd F.R.   MiG-17

Note: served with the 923rd Fighter Regiment.

Tran Cung
Trần Cung
Official Victories: 1

Known Claims
01/07/1969   AQM-34   921st F.R.   MiG-21

Note: Served with the 921st Fighter Regiment.

Tran Hanh
Trần Hanh
Official Victories: 1

Known Claims

04/04/1965	F-105[201]	921st F.R.	Shenyang J-5 2316
06/11/1965	CH-3[202]	921st F.R.	Shenyang J-5 3003

Notes: born on 28/11/1932 in My Loc District, Nam Dinh Province, joined the military in September 1949, trained in the PRC between 1956 and 1964, served with the 921st Fighter Regiment, among the initial group of pilots to land at Phuc Yen on 06/08/1964, was the commander of the 921st Fighter Regiment between 1969 and 1972, became a Deputy Commander of the VPAF in 1972, became Commander of the VPAF in March 1986, was a Deputy Chief of the General Staff of the VPA between 1989 and 1996, was a Deputy Minister of Defence between 1996 and 1999, became a member of the National Assembly and a member of the Central Committee of the Communist Party of Vietnam, assumed a position with the Veteran's Association of Vietnam, attained the rank of Lieutenant General prior to retiring from service in 2000, made Hero of the Vietnam People's Armed Forces on 1 January 1967.

Tran Huyen
Trần Huyền
Official Victories: 2

Known Claims

29/06/1966	2 F-105s[203]	923rd F.R.	MiG-17

---

[201] F-105D 59-1764, 354 TFS, 355 TFW, attached to 2 Air Division, USAF, Captain James A. Magnusson, killed in action.

[202] CH-3C 63-09685, 38 ARRS, USAF, Captain Warren R. Lilly (pilot), prisoner of war, First Lieutenant Jerry A. Singleton, prisoner of war, Staff Sergeant Berkley E. Naugle, recovered, Staff Sergeant Arthur Cormier, prisoner of war. A single VPAF claim was made and shared by Ngo Doan Nhung, Pham Ngoc Lan, Tran Hanh, Tran Minh Phuong.

[203] One of the claims was possibly F-105D 60-0460, 333 TFS, 355 TFW, USAF, Captain Murphy N. Jones, prisoner of war. Two VPAF claims were made and shared by Nguyen Van Bay, Phan Van Tuc, Tran Huyen, Vo Van Man.

| 29/07/1966 | RC-47[204] | 923rd F.R. | MiG-17 |
| 04/12/1966 | F-105 | 923rd F.R. | MiG-17 |

Notes: trained in the PRC, served with the 923rd Fighter Regiment, killed in action on 05/06/1967, attained the rank of Captain.

Tran Minh Phuong

Trần Minh Phương

Official Victories: undetermined

Known Claims

| 06/11/1965 | CH-3[205] | 921st F.R. | MiG-17 |

Notes: served with the 921st and 923rd Fighter Regiments, killed in action on 19/05/1967, attained the rank of Captain.

Tran Ngoc Siu

Trần Ngọc Síu

Official Victories: 2

---

[204] RC-47D 43-48388, 606 ACS, 634 CSG, USAF, Captain Robert E. Hoskinson (pilot), missing in action, Major Galileo F. Bossio, missing in action, First Lieutenant Vincent A. Chiarello, killed or died, date unknown, Captain Bernard Conklin, killed or died, date unknown, First Lieutenant Robert J. Di Tommaso, missing in action, Staff Sergeant James S. Hall, killed or died, date unknown, Technical Sergeant John M. Mamiya, killed or died, date unknown, Technical Sergeant Herbert E. Smith, killed or died, date unknown. A single VPAF claim was made and shared by Tran Huyen and Vo Van Man.

[205] CH-3C 63-09685, 38 ARRS, USAF, Captain Warren R. Lilly (pilot), prisoner of war, First Lieutenant Jerry A. Singleton, prisoner of war, Staff Sergeant Berkley E. Naugle, recovered, Staff Sergeant Arthur Cormier, prisoner of war. A single VPAF claim was made and shared by Ngo Doan Nhung, Pham Ngoc Lan, Tran Hanh, Tran Minh Phuong.

Known Claims

07/07/1966	F-105[206]	921st F.R.	MiG-21PFL
08/12/1966	F-105[207]	921st F.R.	MiG-21

Notes: served with the 921st Fighter Regiment, killed in action by friendly fire on 30/09/1967, attained the rank of Captain.

Tran Triem
Trần Triêm
Official Victories: 1

Known Claims

13/07/1966	A-4	923rd F.R.	MiG-17

Notes: served with the 923rd Fighter Regiment, killed in action on 13/07/1966, attained the rank of Senior Lieutenant.

Tran Van Hoa
Trần Văn Hóa
Official Victories: 1

Known Claims

04/02/1969	AQM-34	921st F.R.	MiG-21

Notes: born in 1945 in Son Tinh District, Quang Ngai Province, trained in the USSR, served with the 921st Fighter Regiment, killed in action on 04/02/1969, attained the rank of Ensign.

---

[206] F-105D 59-1741, 354 TFS, 355 TFW, USAF, Captain Jack H. Tomes, prisoner of war.

[207] F-105D 59-1725, 354 TFS, 355 TFW, USAF, Lieutenant Colonel Donald H. Asire, killed in action.

Tran Van Nam

Trần Văn Năm

Official Victories: 2

Known Claims

11/09/1972	F-4	927th F.R.	MiG-21
06/10/1972	F-4[208]	927th F.R.	MiG-21

Note: Served with the 927th Fighter Regiment.

Tran Viet

Trần Việt

Official Victories: 3

Known Claims

02/06/1968	AQM-34[209]	921st F.R.	MiG-21
08/07/1972	F-4[210]	921st F.R.	MiG-21MF 5106
30/09/1972	F-4	921st F.R.	MiG-21
27/12/1972	F-4[211]	921st F.R.	MiG-21PFM 5033

Notes: born in 1946 in An Nhon District, Binh Dinh Province, joined the military in 1965, trained in the USSR, served with the 921st Fighter Regiment, studied at the Gagarin Air Force Academy, was the commander of the 921st Fighter Regiment between 1982 and 1987, attained the rank of

---

[208] F-4E 69-7548, 25 TFS, 8 TFW, USAF, Lieutenant Colonel Robert D. Anderson (pilot), killed in action, First Lieutenant George F. Latella, prisoner of war.

[209] A single VPAF claim was made and shared by Dinh Ton and Tran Viet.

[210] F-4E 69-7563, 4 TFS, 366 TFW, USAF, Lieutenant Colonel R. E. Ross (pilot), recovered, Captain Stanley M. Imaye, recovered.

[211] Possibly F-4E 67-0292, 13 TFS, 432 TRW, USAF, Major Carl H. Jeffcoat (pilot), prisoner of war, First Lieutenant Jack R. Trimble, prisoner of war.

Major General prior to retiring from service in 2007, made Hero of the Vietnam People's Armed Forces.

Truong Cong Thanh
Trương Công Thành
Official Victories: 1

Known Claims

03/07/1970	AQM-34	923rd F.R.	MiG-17
01/05/1974	AQM-34	923rd F.R.	MiG-17

Notes: served with the 923rd Fighter Regiment, killed in action on 01/05/1974, attained the rank of Senior Lieutenant.

Truong Ton
Trương Tôn
Official Victories: 2

Known Claims

25/06/1972	A-7[212]	927th F.R.	MiG-21
24/07/1972	F-4[213]	927th F.R.	MiG-21MF 5117

Note: served with the 927th Fighter Regiment.

Vo Sy Giap
Võ Sỹ Giáp
Official Victories: 1

---

[212] A-7E 157437, VA-22, USN, USS Coral Sea, Lieutenant Geoffrey R. Shumway, killed in action.

[213]Possibly F-4E 66-0369, 421 TFS, 366 TFW, USAF, Captain Samuel A. Hodnett (pilot), recovered, First Lieutenant David M. Fallert, recovered.

Known Claims

23/08/1969	AQM-34	921st F.R.	MiG-21
18/12/1971	F-4[214]	921st F.R.	MiG-21

Notes: born in 1945 in Nghi Xuan District, Ha Tinh Province, gave up university study in the field of education to join the military in 1965, trained in the PRC, served with the 923rd and 921st Fighter Regiments, became engaged to Bui Thi Tham who worked as a doctor at a military hospital, refused to eject so as to prevent the damaged MiG-21 flown from striking Thuong Trung Secondary School on 08/05/1972, was injured in the crash and died of wounds on 11/05/1972, attained the rank of Senior Lieutenant, made Hero of the Vietnam People's Armed Forces.

Vo Van Man

Võ Văn Mẫn

Official Victories: 5

See the biography and known claims listed under The Aces.

Vu Huy Luong

Vũ Huy Lượng

Official Victories: 1

Known Claims

26/03/1967	F-4[215]	923rd F.R.	MiG-17

Notes: served with the 923rd Fighter Regiment, killed in action on 26/03/1967, attained the rank of Lieutenant.

---

[214] F-4D 65-0799, 13 TFS, 432 TRW, USAF, Major W. T. Stanley (pilot), recovered, Captain L. O'Brien, recovered.

[215] F-4C 64-0849, 433 TFS, 8 TFW, USAF, Lieutenant Colonel Frederick A. Crow (pilot), prisoner of war, First Lieutenant Henry P. Fowler, prisoner of war.

Vu Ngoc Dinh

Vũ Ngọc Đỉnh

Official Victories: 6

See the biography and known claims listed under The Aces.

Vu Nhu Ngu

Vũ Như Ngư

Official Victories: undetermined

Known Claims

27/07/1969   AQM-34   921st F.R.   MiG-21

Note: served with the 921st Fighter Regiment.

Vu The Xuan

Vũ Thế Xuân

Official Victories: 1

Known Claims

19/12/1967   F-105   923rd F.R.   MiG-17F 2077

Note: born in Nam Truc District, Nam Dinh Province, served with the 923rd Fighter Regiment.

Vu Van Dang

Vũ Văn Đang

Official Victories: 1

Known Claims

23/05/1972   F-4[216]   923rd F.R.   MiG-17

---

[216] A single VPAF claim was made and shared by Nguyen Van Dien and Vu Van Dang.

Known Claims
23/05/1972   F-4[216]   923rd F.R.   MiG-17

Notes: served with the 923rd Fighter Regiment, killed in action on 23/05/1972, attained the rank of Senior Lieutenant.

Vu Van Hop
Vũ Văn Hợp
Official Victories: 1

Known Claims
10/05/1972   F-4[217]   927th F.R.   MiG-21
Notes: born on 22 June 1948 in Yen Mo District, Ninh Binh Province, joined the military in 1960, trained in the USSR, served with the 927th Fighter Regiment, killed in action on 08/07/1972, attained the rank of Lieutenant.

Vu Van Ngu
Vũ Văn Ngữ
Official Victories: 1

Known Claims
30/01/1970   AQM-34 921st F.R.   MiG-21

Note: served with the 921st Fighter Regiment.

Vu Xuan Thieu
Vũ Xuân Thi`êu
Official Victories: 1

---

[216] A single VPAF claim was made and shared by Nguyen Van Dien and Vu Van Dang.

[217] F-4J 155800, VF-96, USN, USS Constellation, Lieutenant Randall H. Cunningham (pilot), recovered, Lieutenant Junior Grade William P. Driscoll, recovered.

Known Claims

28/12/1972   B-52   927th F.R.   MiG-21MF 5146

Notes: born in February 1945 in Hai Hau District, Nam Dinh Province, joined the military in 1965, trained in the USSR, served with the 921st and 927th Fighter Regiments, killed in action on 28/12/1972, attained the rank of Captain, made Hero of the Vietnam People's Armed Forces on 20 December 1994.

Appendix II
Claims Of Group Z

The pilots of Group Z claimed several victories, apparently a total of 26, however, specific details of the claims are but few. Known claims of aerial victories, whether subsequently confirmed or not, are listed with the following information: the date of the claim, the aircraft type believed shot down, the pilot to make the claim (if known) and the unit served with when the claim was made, the aircraft in which the claim was made. Note that, while it is believed that the types flown were the Shenyang J-5 and the MiG-21F-13, specific airframes have not been identified. Footnotes include information in respect of the aircraft and crew attacked and regarding the sharing of a claim.

Known Claims

24/04/1967	F-4	Group Z, 923rd F.R.	Shenyang J-5
30/05/1967	A-4[218]	Group Z, 921st F.R.	MiG-21F-13
23/08/1967	F-4	Group Z, 923rd F.R.	Shenyang J-5
16/012/1967	F-4[219]	Group Z, 921st F.R.	MiG-21F-13
05/01/1968	F-105[220]	Group Z, 921st F.R.	MiG-21F-13
18/01/1968	2 F-4s[221]	Group Z, 923rd F.R.	Shenyang J-5(s)
12/02/1968	F-4	Kim Ghi Hoan, Group Z, 923rd F.R.	MiG-21F-13

---

[218] Possibly A-4E 151049, VA-93, USN, USS Hancock, Commander James P. Mehl, prisoner of war.

[219] F-4D 66-7631, 555 TFS, 8TFW, USAF, Major James F. Low (pilot), prisoner of war, First Lieutenant Howard J. Hill, prisoner of war. A single claim was made and shared by two pilots of Doan Z flying MiG-21s of the 921st Fighter Regiment.

[220] F-105F 63-8356, 357 TFS, 355 TFW, USAF, Major James C. Hartney (pilot), killed in action, Captain Samuel Fantle III, killed in action.

[221] F-4D 66-8720, 435 TFS, TFW, USAF, Major Kenneth A. Simonet, (pilot), prisoner of war, First Lieutenant Wayne O. Smith, prisoner of war and F-4D 66-7581, 435 TFS, 8 TFW, USAF, Captain Robert B. Hinckley (pilot), prisoner of war, First Lieutenant Robert C. Jones, prisoner of war.

23/02/1968   F-4D[222] Group Z, 921st F.R.   MiG-21F-13

---

[222] F-4D, 66-8725, 497 TFS, 8 TFW, USAF, Major Laird Gutterson (pilot), prisoner of war, First Lieutenant Myron L. Donald, prisoner of war. A single VPAF claim was made and shared by Hoang Bieu and pilots of the DPRK of Group Z flying MiG-21s of the 921st Fighter Regiment.

Bibliography

Books

Appy, Christian G., Patriots The Vietnam War Remembered From All Sides, Penguin Group, New York, 2003

Boniface, Roger, MiGs Over North Vietnam, Hikoki Publications Ltd., Manchester, 2008

Burgess, Colin and Bert Vis, Interkosmos, Springer published in association with Praxis Publishing, Chichester, 2016

Correll, John T., The Air Force In The Vietnam War, Aerospace Education Foundation, Arlington, 2004

Cony, Christophe and Michel Ledet with Lucien Morareau, L'aviation française en Indochine des origins à 1945, Editions Lela Presse, Outreau, 2012

Davies, Peter, F-4 Phantom II Vs MiG-21, Osprey Publishing, Botley, 2008

Davies, Peter, USN F-4 Phantom II Vs VPAF MiG-17/19, Osprey Publishing, Botley, 2009

Davies, Peter, USAF F-105 Thunderchief Vs VPAF MiG-17, Osprey Publishing, Oxford, 2019

Drendel, Lou, ...And Kill Migs, squadron/signal publications, Warren, 1974

Eden, Paul and Soph Moeng, eds., The Encyclopedia Of World Aircraft, Amber Books Ltd, London, 2002

Ellsberg, Daniel, Secrets: A Memoir Of Vietnam And The Pentagon Papers, The Penguin Group, Toronto, 2003

Ethel, Jeffrey and Alfred Price, One Day In A Long War, Guild Publishing, London, 1990

Francillon, René J., Vietnam Air Wars, The Hamlyn Publishing Group Limited, Twickenham, 1987

Gordon, Yefim, Mikoyan-Gurevich MiG-17, Midland Publishing, Hinckley, 2002

Gordon, Yefim, Mikoyan-Gurevich MiG-19, Midland Publishing, Hinckley, 2003

Gordon, Yefim, and Keith Dexter with Dmitriy Komissarov, Mikoyan MiG-21, Midland Publishing, Hinckley, 2008

Gordon, Yefim and Dmitriy Komissarov, Chinese Aircraft China's aviation industry since 1951, Hikoki Publications, Manchester, 2008

Gordon, Yefim and Dmitriy Komissarov, Soviet and Russian Military Aircraft in Asia, Hikoki Publications, Manchester, 2014

Gordon, Yefim, and Dmitriy Komissarov, Mikoyan MiG-17, Hikoki Publications, Manchester, 2016

Gordon, Yefim, and Dmitriy Komissarov, Mikoyan MiG-19, Hikoki Publications, Manchester, 2017

Hershberger, Mary, Jane Fonda's War, The New Press, New York, 2005

Hallion, Richard P., Rolling Thunder 1965-68 Johnson's air war over Vietnam, Osprey Publishing, Oxford, 2018

Hitchens, Christopher, The Trial Of Henry Kissinger, Twelve, Hachette Book Group, Inc., New York, 2012

Hobson, Chris, Vietnam Air Losses, Midland Publishing, Hinckley, 2001

Lawrence, Mark Atwood, The Vietnam War, Oxford University Press, New York, 2008

McMahon, Robert J., The Limits Of Empire, Columbia University Press, New York, 1999

Maldenov, Alexander, Mikoyan-Gurevich MiG-21, Osprey Publishing, Oxford, 2014

Maldenov, Alexander, Soviet Cold War Fighters, Foothill Media Limited, Oxford, 2016

Mesko, Jim, The South Vietnamese Air Force 1945-1975, squadron/signal Publications, Carrollton, 1987

Mersky, Peter, F-8 Crusader vs MiG-17, Osprey Publishing, Oxford, 2014

Michel III, Marshall L., Clashes, Naval Institute Press, Annapolis, 1997

Michel III, Marshall L., The 11 Days Of Christmas, Encounter Books, New York, 2002

Michel III, Marshall L., Operation Linebacker II 1972 The B-52s are sent to Hanoi, Osprey Publishing, Oxford, 2018

Michel III, Marshall L., Operation Linebacker I 1972 The first high-tech air war, Osprey Publishing, Oxford, 2019

Nguyễn Đức Soát and Nguyễn Sỹ Hưng, Chiến Tranh Trên Không Ở Việt
    Nam (1965-1973) Phía Sau Những Trận Không Chiến, Nhà Xuất Bản
    Quân Đội Nhân Dân, Hà Nội, 2017
Nguyễn Sỹ Hưng and Nguyễn Nam Liên, Những Trận Không Chiến Trên Bầu
    Trời Việt Nam (1965-1975) Nhìn Từ Hai Phía, Nhà Xuất Bản Quân
    Đội Nhân Dân, Hà Nội, 2014
Nichols, John B., and Barrett Tillman, On Yankee Station, Airlife Publishing,
    Shrewsbury, 1987
Noreen, Lon O., Air Warfare In The Missile Age, Second Edition, The
    Smithsonian Institution, Washington, 2002
Olynk, Frank, Stars & Bars, Grub Street, London, 1995
Paloque, Gérard, The Mikoyan-Gurevitch [sic] «Fishbed» (1955-2010),
    histoire & collections, Paris, 2009
Price, Alfred, Sky Warriors, Arms And Armour, London, 1994
Shores, Christopher, Fighter Aces, The Hamlyn Publishing Group Limited,
    Feltham, 1975
Sutiagin, Yuri and Igor Seidov, MiG Menace Over Korea, Pen & Sword
    Aviation, Barnsley, 2009
Toperczer, István, Air War Over North Viet Nam, squadron/signal
    publications, Carrollton, 1998
Toperczer, István, MiG-17 And 19 Units Of The Vietnam War, Osprey
    Publishing, Botley, 2001
Toperczer, István, MiG-21 Units Of The Vietnam War, Osprey Publishing,
    Botley, 2001
Toperczer, István, MiG Aces of the Vietnam War, Schiffer Publishing Ltd.,
    Atglen, 2015
Toperczer, István, Silver Swallows And Blue Bandits, Artipresse, Bagnolet,
    2015
Toperczer, István, MiG-17/19 Aces Of The Vietnam War, Osprey Publishing,
    Oxford, 2016
Toperczer, István, MiG-21 Aces Of The Vietnam War, Osprey Publishing,
    Oxford, 2016
Van Staaveren, Jacob, Gradual Failure The Air War Over North Vietnam
    1965-1966, United States Air Force, Washington, 2002
Wiest, Andrew, ed., Rolling Thunder In A Gentle Land, Osprey Publishing,
    Botley, 2006

Articles

Buza, Zoltán, MiG-17 over Vietnam, Wings Of Fame, Volume 8, Aerospace
    Publishing Ltd, London, 1997

Buza, Zoltán and István Toperczer, MiG-19 in Vietnam, Wings Of Fame,
    Volume 11, Aerospace Publishing Ltd, London, 1998

Michel, Marshall L., The Xmas Bombing, Air & Space Smithsonian
    Collector's Edition 2015, Smithsonian Enterprises, Washington,
    Summer, 2015

Nguyen, Binh, Chiến tích siêu đẳng của phi công Việt Nam chuyên săn diệt
    F-4, netNEWS, 08/01/2016

O'Conner, Michael, Duel Over The Dragon's Jaw, AAHS Journal, Volume 25,
    Number 4 Winter 1980, American Aviation Historical Society,
    Santa Ana, 1980

Olds, Robin, Forty Six Years a Fighter Pilot, AAHS Journal, Volume 13,
    Number 4 Winter 1968, American Aviation Historical Society, Los
    Angeles, 1968

Phạm Ánh Tuyết, Khoang đổ bộ tàu Liên hợp 37 và chuyến du hành vũ trụ
    của anh hùng Phạm Tuân, Bảo tàng Lịch sử Quân sự Việt Nam,
    29/06/2018

Phan Nguyệt, Vùng trời kỷ niệm, Cao Bằng Online, 29/12/2012

Phương Bình, Trọn nghĩa, vẹn tình, Phòng không - Không quân, 29/08/2018

Schuster, Carl O., The Rise of North Vietnam's Air Defenses, Vietnam,
    HistoryNet, June, 2016, Vol. 29, No. 1

Trương Thanh Tùng, Nguyễn Văn Bảy, lão nông anh hùng từng bắn rơi 7
    máy bay Mỹ, zing.vn, 23/09/2019

Wetterhahn, Ralph, Nguyen Van Bay and the Aces From the North, Air &
    Space Smithsonian Collector's Edition 2015, Smithsonian
    Enterprises, Washington, Summer, 2015

Recordings

MiG 17 Pilot Nguyen Van Bay and Photographer Nick Ut, Peter Scheid Film
    & Photography

Nguyễn Hồng Mỹ and John L. Styles, interviewed by John Mollison, The
    History Lesson

MiG-21PFM 4326, serial 772111, of the 921st Fighter Regiment, flown by several pilots of the VPAF to claim 13 aircraft destroyed, respected in repose at the Air Defence - Air Force Museum in Hanoi.

Printed in Great Britain
by Amazon